AF156594

JOBBASICS A2

Englisch für berufliche Schulen

von
Jingyun Liu
Michael Macfarlane
Will McNeice
Petra Schappert
Isobel Williams

in Zusammenarbeit mit
der Verlagsredaktion

Cornelsen

Verfasser/innen:	Jingyun Liu
	Michael Macfarlane
	Will McNeice
	Petra Schappert
	Isobel Williams

Berater/innen: Marco Henkel, Geislingen

Projektleitung:	Jim Austin
Verlagsredaktion:	Shaunessy Ashdown
Außenredaktion:	Birgit Reinel
Redaktionelle Mitarbeit:	Simone Conrad, Christine House, Andreas Hug, Christiane Knudsen, Simone Neumann, John Stevens, Oliver Busch (Wörterverzeichnisse)
Bildredaktion:	Gertha Maly
Umschlaggestaltung, Layout und technische Umsetzung:	vitaledesign, Berlin
Illustrationen:	Oxford Designers & Illustrators

Erhältlich sind auch:

Handreichungen für den Unterricht mit CD-ROM und Audio-CD   ISBN 978-3-06-450697-8

www.cornelsen.de

Die Webseiten Dritter, deren Internetadressen in diesem Lehrwerk angegeben sind, wurden vor Drucklegung sorgfältig geprüft. Der Verlag übernimmt keine Gewähr für die Aktualität und den Inhalt dieser Seiten oder solcher, die mit ihnen verlinkt sind.

1. Auflage, 4. Druck 2022

Alle Drucke dieser Auflage sind inhaltlich unverändert und können im Unterricht nebeneinander verwendet werden.

© 2012 Cornelsen Verlag, Berlin
© 2018 Cornelsen Verlag GmbH, Berlin

Das Werk und seine Teile sind urheberrechtlich geschützt. Jede Nutzung in anderen als den gesetzlich zugelassenen Fällen bedarf der vorherigenschriftlichen Einwilligung des Verlages. Hinweis zu §§ 60a, 60b UrhG: Weder das Werk noch seine Teile dürfen ohne eine solche Einwilligung an Schulen oder in Unterrichts- und Lehrmedien (§ 60b Abs. 3 UrhG) vervielfältigt, insbesondere kopiert oder eingescannt, verbreitet oder in ein Netzwerk eingestellt oder sonst öffentlich zugänglich gemacht oder wiedergegeben werden. Dies gilt auch für Intranets von Schulen.

Druck: Athesiadruck GmbH

ISBN 978-3-06-450696-1 (Schülerbuch)
ISBN 978-3-06-450739-5 (E-Book)

PEFC zertifiziert
Dieses Produkt stammt aus nachhaltig bewirtschafteten Wäldern und kontrollierten Quellen.

PEFC™
PEFC/18-31-166   www.pefc.de

Liebe Lernende, liebe Kolleginnen und Kollegen,

- Mit **Job Basics A2** lernen die Schülerinnen und Schüler, berufsbezogen auf Englisch zu handeln, und erleben Freude daran, die Sprache sofort in realistischen Kontexten anzuwenden.
- **Job Basics A2** eignet sich für Auszubildende aller Berufsfelder, die ihre Kompetenzen in Englisch auf Niveau A2 (GER) auf berufliche Inhalte anwenden und weiterentwickeln wollen.
- **Job Basics A2** ist für alle beruflichen Schulen geeignet.
- Der größte Teil des Buchs ist in *Situation Blocks* und *Scenarios* unterteilt, die in beliebiger Reihenfolge bearbeitet werden können.
  - Innerhalb der *Situation Blocks* werden *38 Situations* – jeweils auf einer Doppelseite – angeboten, die in etwa einer Unterrichtsstunde erarbeitet werden können.
  - Die *Scenarios* führen wichtige Strukturen und Elemente in berufsbezogenen Handlungen zusammen.
- **Job Basics A2** bereitet auf die *KMK-Prüfung* (Stufe I) vor. Speziell gekennzeichnete Übungen kommen punktuell vor, ebenso wie *Exam Practice*-Seiten, die nach Kompetenzen (Lese- und Hörverstehen, Produktion, Mediation und Interaktion) sortiert sind. Auch eine vollständige Musterprüfung ist enthalten.
- **Job Basics A2** erleichtert die Arbeit mit unterschiedlichen Leistungsniveaus und bietet viele Aufgaben zur Binnendifferenzierung.
- **Job Basics A2** motiviert die Lernenden dazu, bereits vorhandene Englischkenntnisse berufsbezogen anzuwenden. Die berufspraktische Relevanz des Fachs Englisch wird durch die Vielfalt an Beispielen aus allen Berufsrichtungen deutlich.
- **Job Basics A2** stellt auch Richtlinien für das Verfassen von E-Mails, Geschäftsbriefen und einen Lebenslauf nach Europass-Standard zur Verfügung. In den *Partner Files* gibt es zahlreiche Rollenkarten. Ein *Extra Reading*-Teil stellt interessante Textlektionen zur Verfügung.
- **Job Basics A2** hält ein umfangreiches Angebot für Lehrende bereit: Die *Handreichungen für den Unterricht* enthalten die Lösungen zu den Aufgaben, die Audio-CDs sowie Transkripte zu den Hörübungen, hilfreiche didaktische Hinweise zu jeder Lektion, eine CD-ROM mit vielen Zusatzmaterialien in Form von editierbaren Kopiervorlagen (auch zu Grammatikthemen), zwei zusätzliche KMK-Musterprüfungen, Vokabelllisten (*basic*, *advanced*, chronologisch nach Lektion) und auch Grafiken aus dem Buch zur Verwendung auf Papier, Folie oder per Beamer.

Im Buch werden folgende Symbole verwendet:

 zu der Übung liegt ein Track auf der Audio-CD vor

 diese Übung entspricht in ihrer Konzeption der KMK-Zertifikatsprüfung

 die Lernenden wählen je nach Kenntnisstand die einfachere ★ oder etwas anspruchsvollere Übung ★★ aus

✈ diese Aufgabe erledigen Lernende, die bereits früher mit den anderen Aufgaben fertig sind

Viel Spaß und Erfolg im Unterricht wünschen

die Autoren, die Berater und der Verlag

TABLE OF CONTENTS

THE SITUATION Jens Meyer works for SonnenPower in Stuttgart. Today he is at the airport. His boss, Ms Schmuck, has asked him to go there to meet a visitor.

1 | Understanding spoken dialogues

1/2

A Hören Sie sich das Gespräch an und beantworten Sie die folgenden Fragen. Es ist in Ordnung, wenn Sie noch nicht alles verstehen!

1   Did Mr Perez expect Jens or Ms Schmuck to meet him?
2   How was Mr Perez's flight?
3   Does Mr Perez let Jens carry all of his bags?
4   How will Jens and Mr Perez leave the airport: by car or by bus?

1/3

B Jens holt häufiger Besucher ab. Hören Sie sich drei Gespräche hierzu an. Stellen Sie fest, ob das Folgende in Gespräch A, B oder C passiert.

1   Jens meets the visitor at the train station.
2   The visitor doesn't let Jens carry her bag.
3   The visitor's plane lands on time.
4   Jens and the visitor leave by car.
5   Jens and the visitor leave by bus.

C Arbeiten Sie mit einem Partner und schreiben Sie für jede der folgenden Fragen zwei mögliche Antworten in Ihr Notizheft.

1   Are you [Name]?
    Yes, I am.
    No, I'm not. Sorry!
2   Did you have a good flight?
3   Can I help you with your bags?
4   Shall we go to the car?

2 | Playing a dialogue

A Benutzen Sie die Rollenkarten auf S. 136–137. Partner A verwendet hierzu File 1, Partner B File 5. Zuerst liest Partner A die Sätze 1–4 vor und Partner B wählt eine passende Antwort aus dem Kästchen aus. Dann wird gewechselt. Üben Sie das Zuhören, indem Sie den Text Ihres Partners nicht mitlesen.

B Spielen Sie die folgende Gesprächssituation durch. Benutzen Sie dazu Ausdrücke aus der ‚Useful language'-Box. Tauschen Sie anschließend die Rollen.

Host

Sprechen Sie B höflich an. Fragen Sie, ob er/sie Herr/Frau Perez ist.

Visitor

Bejahen Sie.

Stellen Sie sich vor.

Reagieren Sie und sagen Sie, dass Sie sich freuen A kennenzulernen.

Erwidern Sie die Phrase. Heißen Sie dann B in Deutschland willkommen.

Danken Sie A dafür, dass er/sie Sie abholt.

Fragen Sie, wie der Flug war.

Antworten Sie.

Bieten Sie an, mit dem Gepäck zu helfen.

Antworten Sie.

Fordern Sie B höflich auf mitzukommen.

USEFUL LANGUAGE

Host
Excuse me, are you *[Name]*?
My name is *[Ihr Name]*.
    I'm from *[Name Ihrer Firma]*.
Nice to meet you.
Welcome to Germany.
Sure. / No problem.
Did you have a good flight?
Can I help you with your bags?
Let's go to the car.

Visitor
Yes, I am. / No, I'm not.
    You have the wrong person!
Nice to meet you.
Thank you for picking me up.
The flight was fine/terrible.
    It was on time/late.
Yes, thank you. / No, thanks.
    I can manage the bags.

C Führen Sie Ihr Gespräch einer anderen Gruppe vor.

THE SITUATION Heike Lull works for SonnenPower in Stuttgart. She is greeting a visitor who has just come from the airport.

1 Understanding dialogues

1/4

A Hören Sie sich das Gespräch an und beantworten Sie die folgenden Fragen.

1 What does Heike say her job is?
   a Ms Schmuck's assistant
   b a technician in Ms Schmuck's department
   c an intern
   d a solar energy specialist

2 Where is Ms Schmuck at the moment?
   a at lunch
   b on holiday
   c in her office
   d on the telephone

3 What does Heike offer the guest?
   a something to drink
   b to wait for Ms Schmuck at the entrance
   c a biscuit
   d a sweet

4 What does the guest ask for?
   a a glass of water
   b to use the telephone
   c the way to the toilet
   d the way to Ms Schmuck's office

1/5

B Hören Sie sich zwei weitere Gespräche an und beantworten Sie dieselben Fragen.

2 Making offers and requests

USEFUL LANGUAGE

Angebote und Bitten
Wenn man etwas anbietet, sagt man …
   Would you like … (a cup of coffee? / to hang up your coat? / etc.)
Wenn man um etwas bittet, sagt man …
   Could I … (have a glass of water, please?)
   Could you … (tell me where the toilet is, please?)

A   Wechseln Sie sich ab und stellen Sie Ihrem Partner Fragen mit *Would you like … ?*, *Could I … ?* und *Could you … ?* Antworten Sie mit den Ausdrücken auf der rechten Seite.

Angebote (Would you like … ?)		Antworten
… to wait here?	→	Sure. Thank you.
… something to drink? Coffee? Water?	→	A glass of water would be nice.
… a biscuit?	→	No, thank you.

Bitten (Could I/you … ?)		Antworten
… tell me where the toilets are, please?	→	Yes, of course. Just down here on the right.
… use the telephone, please?	→	Of course. You can use mine.
… tell me where Ms Schmuck's office is, please?	→	Sure. It's just down here on the left.
… have a glass of water, please?	→	Of course. I'll get you one.

B   Partner A deckt die linke Spalte oben mit der Hand oder einem Blatt Papier ab. Partner B stellt nun in zufälliger Reihenfolge die Fragen. Nachdem Sie alle Fragen gestellt und beantwortet haben, tauschen Sie die Rollen.

3 | Welcoming a visitor/visiting a company

★ A   Die Klasse wird in zwei Gruppen geteilt: Besucher und Gastgeber. Nehmen Sie eine der folgenden Rollen ein: Besucher A, Besucher B, Besucher C, Gastgeber A, Gastgeber B, Gastgeber C. Stellen Sie sich mit Ihrem eigenen Namen vor und stellen Sie die Frage, die zu Ihrer Rolle gehört (siehe unten). Üben Sie mit so vielen Partnern wie möglich. Reagieren Sie auf die Fragen Ihrer Partner.

Visitor A fragt:	'Could you tell me where the lift is, please?'
Visitor B fragt:	'Could I borrow a pen, please?'
Visitor C fragt:	'Could I make a copy on the copy machine, please?'
Host A fragt:	'Would you like me to show you around the offices?'
Host B fragt:	'Would you like to use my computer to check your e-mails?'
Host C fragt:	'Would you like a sweet?'

★★ B   Schreiben Sie selber einige Angebote auf, die Gastgeber machen können, und notieren Sie Bitten und Fragen, die Gäste haben können. Dann benutzen Sie sie in Willkommensgesprächen, wie oben. Machen Sie die Übung mit mehreren Partnern.

THE SITUATION Silke Meyer works for Besterman Systems. She receives this e-mail from her boss, Aykan Sufolgu.

An:	S Meyer
Betreff:	Zarka Engineering Sales Visit
Von:	Aykan Sufolgu · Signatur: Ohne ·

Hi Silke

Mr Gabor Simka, Zarkas's Purchasing Manager, is arriving from Budapest for a meeting at 2.00 p.m. today. The problem is that the meeting I'm having with Auto Elektra in Mannheim won't finish until 1.00 p.m., and I can't get back to the office till 2.30 p.m. So could you please meet him in Reception to apologize and explain the situation? And then would be useful to show him round the company for half an hour.

Thanks!

Aykan

A Lesen Sie die E-Mail und beantworten Sie die folgenden Fragen.

1 Wer ist Gabor Simka, und was macht er heute?
2 Was ist das ‚Problem', das Aykan beschreibt?
3 Worum bittet Aykan?

B Schreiben Sie gemeinsam mit einem Partner auf Englisch eine Beschreibung des Fotos nieder.

1 Understanding a company tour

A Ordnen Sie die Piktogramme A–H ihren englischen Bezeichnungen 1–8 zu. Nennen Sie die deutschen Bezeichnungen.

1	Accounts	3	IT	5	R & D	7	Training Centre
2	Cafeteria	4	Customer Service	6	Sales	8	Warehouse

1/6

B Schauen Sie sich die drei möglichen Rundgänge durch die Firma an. Hören Sie den Text und finden Sie heraus, welchen Rundgang Silke macht. Für welchen Ort interessiert sich Gabor Simka am meisten und wie drückt er das aus?

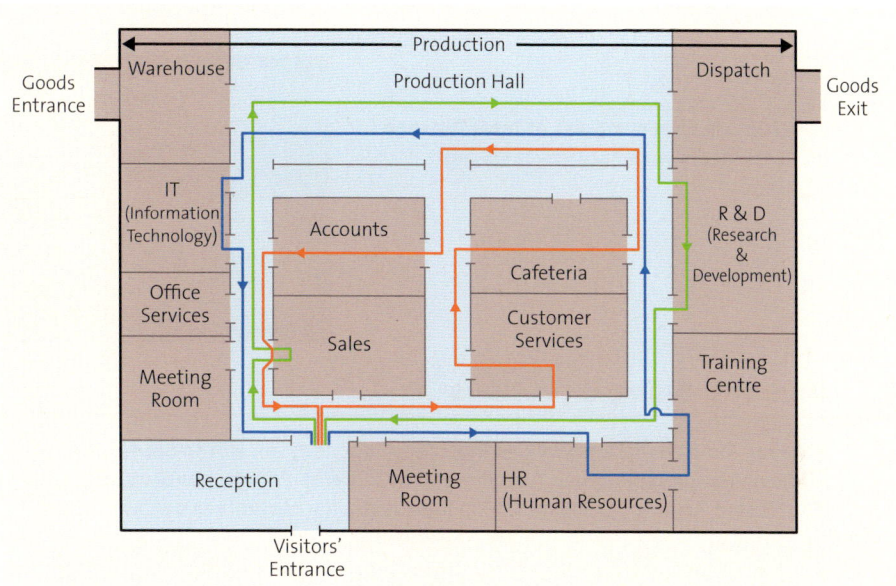

1/7

C Hören Sie sich einen weiteren Rundgang an, dieses Mal mit einem anderen Kollegen und einem anderen Besucher. Welcher Rundgang ist es (Rot, Grün oder Blau)? Welcher Ort interessiert diesen Besucher besonders? Wie drückt er das aus?

2 | Giving a company tour

A Die folgenden acht Sätze werden bei Rundgängen häufig verwendet. Hören Sie sich noch einmal Rundgang 2 an. Welchen Satz hören Sie jeweils – a oder b?

1 a Let's go in here.
  b Let's go this way.
2 a Here we have Sales on the right.
  b This is Sales on the left.
3 a And now you can see Dispatch on our left.
  b And now we can see Dispatch on our right.
4 a Next let's take a look at the Accounts department.
  b Let's walk through the department.

B Partnerarbeit: Tun Sie so, als gingen Sie und Ihr Partner mit einem Besucher auf dem roten Rundgang. Verwenden Sie die Sätze aus Aufgabe A.

C Zeichnen Sie beide einen einfachen Plan (eines Teils) Ihres Arbeitsplatzes. Kennzeichnen Sie jeweils zwei oder drei Stellen, aber lassen Sie drei oder vier für Ihren Partner frei. Sollten Sie eine Bezeichnung auf Englisch nicht kennen, fragen Sie Ihren Lehrer.

D Tauschen Sie Ihre Pläne aus. Machen Sie mit Ihrem Partner dann einen Rundgang durch Ihren Arbeitsplatz und lassen Sie ihn die leeren Stellen ausfüllen.

E Wiederholen Sie die Rundgänge. Diesmal soll der Gast Fragen stellen und Interesse zeigen (wie Gabor Simka). Der Gastgeber soll auf die Kommentare und Fragen antworten.

> **THE SITUATION**
>
> Alex Klein is a receptionist at InterTec, and he often deals with English-speaking visitors.

1 Understanding directions

1/8

Schauen Sie sich die Ansicht des InterTec-Gebäudes an. Hören Sie sich an, wie Alex den Weg zu vier verschiedenen Abteilungen beschreibt *(Customer Services, Sales, Training Centre* und *Accounts)*. Notieren Sie jeweils die Raumnummer der Abteilung.

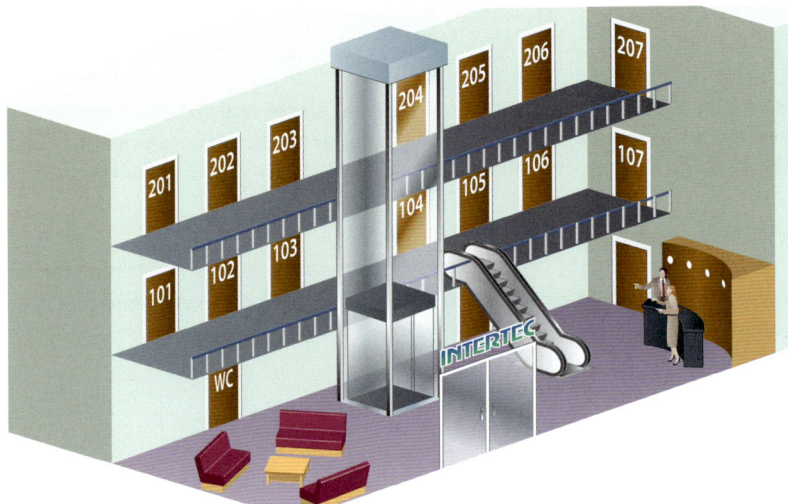

CULTURE

Männer werden immer mit *Mr* angeredet, egal, ob sie verheiratet sind oder nicht. Bei Frauen verwendet man analog die Anrede *Ms.* Wenn bekannt ist, dass eine Frau den Nachnamen ihres Ehemannes angenommen hat, verwendet man *Mrs.*
Wenn Sie diese verheirateten Frauen treffen würden, würden Sie *Ms ...* oder *Mrs ...* sagen?

... Jolie   ... Obama   ... Beckham   ... Shriver

2 | Giving directions

Take the	escalator lift		to the	first second	floor.
Go upstairs					
Turn	left right	and go		along the to the end of the	corridor.
It's the	first second last	door		on your you come to.	left. right.

A Spielen Sie mit einem Partner Alex' Gespräche durch. Verwenden Sie dazu die Ausdrücke aus der ‚Useful language'-Box.

Alex   And now please go up to room …
Visitor   Thanks. But can you tell me the way, please?
Alex   Of course. First, … . Then you … . And it's …
Visitor   So first I have to … . Then I … . And it's …
Alex   That's right.

B Verbessern Sie Alex' Angaben.

Alex   So now could you go up to room 202, Ms Stefano?
Ms S   Can you tell me how to get there, please?
Alex   First, take the escalator to the first floor. Then you turn right and go to the end of the corridor. And it's the last door you come to.

C Erstellen Sie neue Dialoge für weitere Besucher.

Name: Herr Takeshi Honda   **Name:** Dr Maria Nevski
Ziel: Raum 205   **Ziel:**   Raum 105

D Einige der Besucher brauchen noch eine Wegbeschreibung zu einem zweiten Meeting bei InterTec. Arbeiten Sie mit einem Partner und verwenden Sie für Ihre Dialoge die Rollenkarten.

1   Frau Kramer muss von Raum 101 zu Raum 203.

★   Die Rollenkarte für Frau Kramer finden Sie in File 2 auf S. 136.

★★   Die Rollenkarte für den Angestellten in Raum 101 finden Sie in File 6 auf S. 137.

2   Frau Stefano muss von Raum 206 zu Raum 305.

★   Die Rollenkarte für Frau Stefano finden Sie in File 9 auf S. 138.

★★   Die Rollenkarte für den Angestellten in Raum 206 finden Sie in File 12 auf S. 139.

YOUR CHOICE

THE SITUATION

Suzan Evren works for AutoElektra, and she is a security officer at the main entrance. She checks deliveries, and the truck drivers often need directions to different parts of the company. She often has to give these in English.

1   Understanding directions

1/9

Staff Health Centre • Dispatch • Factory Goods Entrance • Storage Rooms • Training Centre • R & D

A   Hören Sie, wie Suzan vier Fahrern den Weg zu den oben genannten Orten beschreibt, die auf der Karte mit A–F gekennzeichnet sind. Notieren Sie die Namen für die Orte A-F.

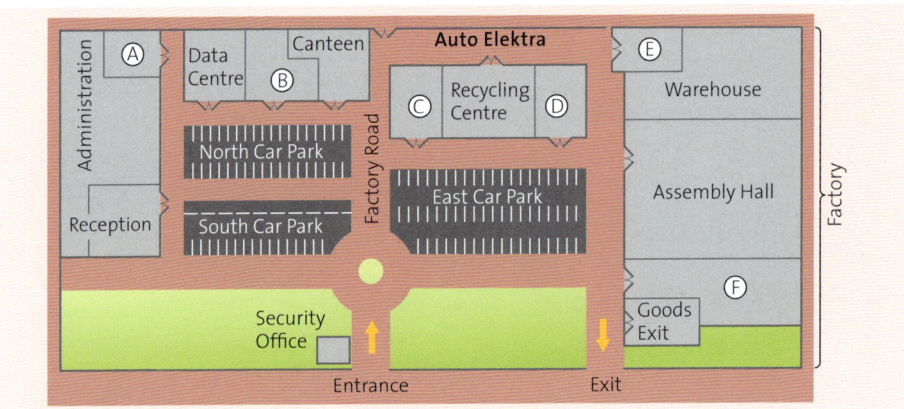

B   Übertragen Sie Suzans Anlieferungsregister in Ihr Heft und fügen Sie drei weitere Zeilen hinzu. Hören Sie sich die Gespräche noch einmal an und vervollständigen Sie das Register. Achten Sie besonders auf die folgenden Begriffe, um die Spalte ‚Description of goods' ausfüllen zu können. Schauen Sie auf eine Uhr in Ihrem Klassenraum, damit Sie die Anlieferungszeit jedes Postens hinzufügen können.

computer monitors • electrical components • fitness equipment • a large machine • office furniture • packing materials

	Delivery destination	Description of goods	Time of delivery
1	*Storage Rooms*	*office furniture*	...

2 | Giving directions

Can I see your paperwork, please?
It's a load of …
I have to deliver to … . Can you tell me the way?
No problem. First, … . Then you … . It's …
OK, so first I need to … . Then I … . And it's …

Turn	Go over left at right at	the roundabout, and drive		straight on. past …

Take the	first second third	left right	and you'll see it	in front of you. on	the your	left. right.

next to …
opposite …
between … and …

A Einige der LKW-Fahrer fahren aus Versehen zu den falschen Orten. Nehmen Sie mit einem Partner jeweils die Position des Fahrers und des AutoElektra-Angestellten vor Ort ein. Verwenden Sie die Karte auf S. 14. Beginnen Sie Ihre Dialoge wie folgt:

YOUR CHOICE

Driver   Excuse me. Can you tell me … , please?
Employee   No problem. You need to go back past … . Then go … . And you'll see it …

1 Location now: Staff Health Centre
    Delivery destination: Storage Rooms

2 Location now: Storage Rooms
    Delivery destination: R & D

B Führen Sie in Partnerarbeit weitere Dialoge zwischen zwei verschiedenen Fahrern und einem Pförtner. Verwenden Sie dazu das folgende Anlieferungsregister, den Lageplan in 1A und die ‚Useful language'-Box.

	Delivery destination	Description of goods	Time of delivery
1	R & D (C)	a large machine	…
2	Factory Goods Entrance (E)	electrical components	…

C Wählen Sie mit Ihrem Partner einen weitläufigen Ort mit mehreren Gebäuden, den Sie beide gut kennen, z. B. Ihren Arbeitsplatz, Ihr Schulgelände oder ein örtliches Einkaufszentrum. Wechseln Sie sich mit den Rollen eines Besuchers und eines Angestellten, die am Eingang stehen, ab. Fragen Sie nach dem Weg bzw. beschreiben Sie den Weg zu verschiedenen Orten.

THE SITUATION Freja Hoyem is coming to InterTec for a job interview. The company has sent her directions which explain how to get to their offices from the train station.

1 Understanding written directions

A Lesen Sie die E-Mail und suchen Sie das Büro von InterTec, in dem das Vorstellungsgespräch stattfinden soll, auf der Karte.

Dear Ms Hoyem

Our offices are only a short walk from the station. Here are some directions to help you find us.

Leave the station by the east exit and turn right into Oststrasse. Then take the first left into Kapelstrasse. Go straight down the hill, past a post office on your left and a police station on your right. At the bottom of the hill, take a short cut through a small park across the road. When you come to the pond at the centre of the park, turn left and walk round it until you come to a restaurant. There you turn left, away from the pond and walk to the exit. Then you need to turn left at a supermarket and take the first right. You will find our offices 50 metres along the street on the right, just behind the supermarket.

We look forward to seeing you here at 3.00 p.m. on Monday 17th October.

Yours sincerely

Barbara Benitez
Assistant Manager, Human Resources

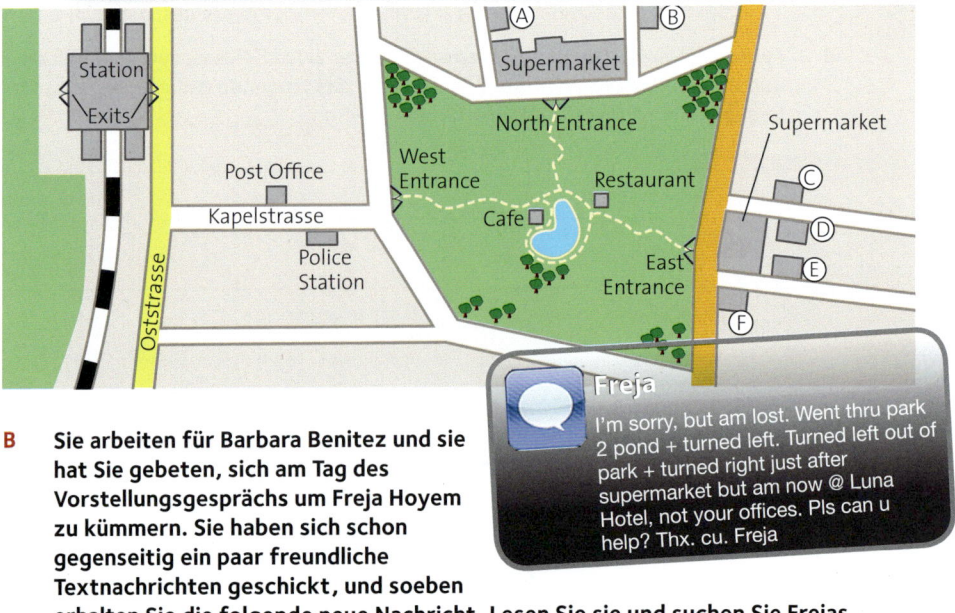

B Sie arbeiten für Barbara Benitez und sie hat Sie gebeten, sich am Tag des Vorstellungsgesprächs um Freja Hoyem zu kümmern. Sie haben sich schon gegenseitig ein paar freundliche Textnachrichten geschickt, und soeben erhalten Sie die folgende neue Nachricht. Lesen Sie sie und suchen Sie Frejas Standort auf der Karte.

> **Freja**
> I'm sorry, but am lost. Went thru park 2 pond + turned left. Turned left out of park + turned right just after supermarket but am now @ Luna Hotel, not your offices. Pls can u help? Thx. cu. Freja

C Ordnen Sie jeder der unten stehenden Abkürzungen ihre passende Bedeutung zu.

1	thru	5	@	a	you	e	and
2	2	6	pls	b	at	f	see you
3	+	7	thx	c	thanks	g	to
4	u	8	cu	d	through	h	please

2 | Giving written directions

A Verwenden Sie Frejas Textnachricht, um eine formelle E-Mail an Frau Benitez zu verfassen. Bilden Sie vollständige Sätze und machen Sie aus den Abkürzungen ganze Wörter. Beginnen Sie so:

> Dear Ms Benitez
> Ms Hoyem has sent me this message:
> I am sorry, but I am lost. I went ...

B Fügen Sie jetzt eine Erklärung für Frejas falschen Weg hinzu. Beginnen Sie so:

> It is clear she did not turn left at the right place. I think she took the first ... and not the ..., and I think she exited the park from ...

C Verwenden Sie die Karte und die ursprüngliche E-Mail von Barbara Benitez, um Freja mit einer Textnachricht zu antworten. Beschreiben Sie ihr den Weg von dort aus, wo sie jetzt gerade ist. Versuchen Sie, einige Abkürzungen aus der Liste in 1C zu verwenden.

REMEMBER

She **turned** left at the wrong place.
She **did not turn** left at the right place.
(Unregelmäßige Vergangenheitsformen der Verben finden Sie auf der Innenseite des hinteren Buchumschlags.)

★★ D Beschreiben Sie in einer geschäftlichen E-Mail an einen wichtigen Geschäftspartner den Weg vom Hotel Luna (A) zum Bahnhof.

★ E Schreiben Sie eine informelle Textnachricht an einen Geschäftspartner, den Sie gut kennen, in der Sie den Weg von Punkt E (einem Bürogebäude) auf der Karte in 1A zum Bahnhof beschreiben. Verwenden Sie dazu Abkürzungen, wie sie in Textnachrichten üblich sind.

YOUR
CHOICE

✈ F Beschreiben Sie in einer E-Mail an einen Freund den Weg von einem Bahnhof oder einer Bushaltestelle in Ihrem Wohnort zu Ihrer Schule oder Ihrem Arbeitsplatz.

THE SITUATION Various visitors are in town and are asking local people for directions. The visitors are: a patient at a doctor's office, two tourists, a shopper and a truck driver.

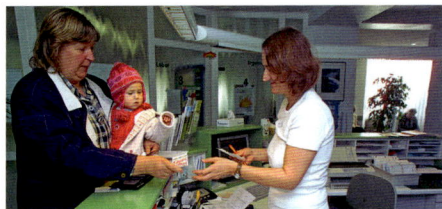

At the City Clinic

At the City Hotel

At the City Shopping Centre

At the City Business Park

1 Following directions

A Schauen Sie sich die Karte an und finden Sie möglichst viele der folgenden Orte.

castle	Burg/Schloss	museum	Museum
department store	Kaufhaus	petrol station	Tankstelle
hospital	Krankenhaus	pharmacy	Apotheke
industrial estate	Gewerbegebiet	shoe shop	Schuhgeschäft

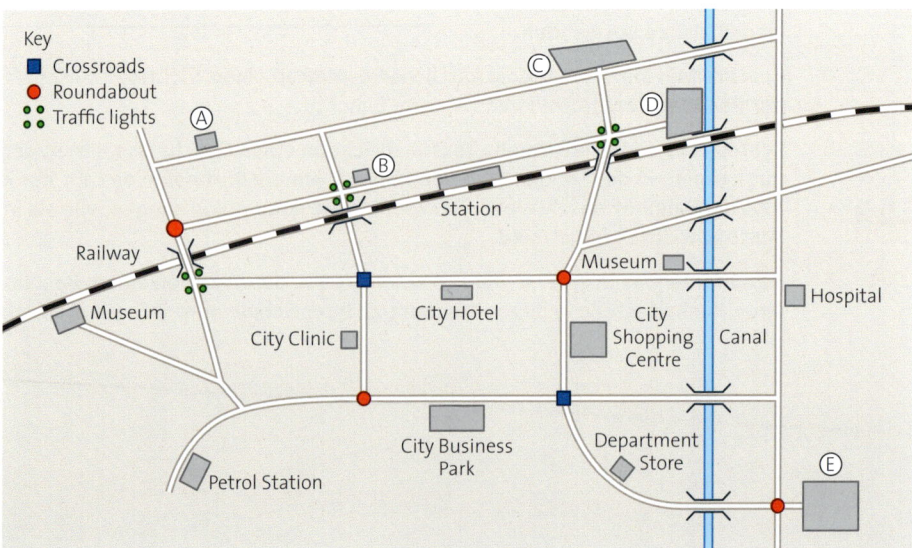

B Hören Sie sich Gespräch 1 in der Klinik an und folgen Sie dem Weg der Familie zu ihrem Ziel – A, B, C, D oder E. Übertragen Sie zuvor die folgende Tabelle in Ihr Heft und verwenden Sie diese für Ihre Notizen. Lassen Sie unten etwas Platz für weitere Notizen.

1/10

Conversation	Visitors	Leaving from	Going to	
			Letter A–E	Location name
1	*the patient*	*the City ...*	*...*	*the ...*

C Hören Sie sich die Gespräche 2–4 an. Stellen Sie zuerst fest, wer und wo die Besucher sind. Hören Sie die Gespräche dann noch einmal und folgen Sie den Wegen nach A, B, C, D oder E. Tragen Sie Ihre neuen Notizen unten in der Tabelle aus 1B ein.

1/11

2 Giving directions

A Schauen Sie sich die Bilder 1–6 an. Suchen Sie dann mit einem Partner die nötigen Richtungshinweise aus der ‚Useful language'-Box heraus.

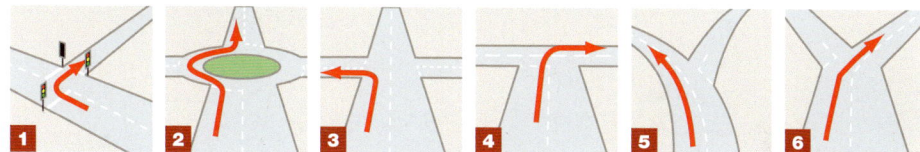

B Wechseln Sie sich mit einem Partner ab und fragen Sie sich gegenseitig nach dem Weg zu verschiedenen Orten auf der Karte auf S. 18. Wählen Sie dazu die Orte A–E als Ausgangspunkte und beschreiben Sie von dort aus den Weg zu den folgenden Zielen:

Käufer: vom Schuhgeschäft zum Kaufhaus
Touristen: von der Burg zum Museum in der Nähe der Bahngleise
Patient: von der Apotheke zum Krankenhaus
LKW-Fahrer: vom Gewerbegebiet zur Tankstelle

C Bilden Sie Gruppen. Jeder schreibt den Namen eines in Ihrer Region bekannten Ziels auf einen Zettel. Das Ziel sollte nicht zu weit weg liegen und mit dem Auto (oder dem Fahrrad) erreichbar sein. Die Zettel bleiben verdeckt. Nachdem der erste den Weg zu seinem geheimen Ziel beschrieben hat, dürfen alle einmal raten, was es ist. Errät jemand, was auf dem Zettel steht? Danach kommt der Nächste dran.

USEFUL LANGUAGE

Turn right/left out of the car park.

		the crossroads.
	Go over	the roundabout.
		the traffic lights.
Turn/Go	left at	the fork.
	right at	the T-intersection.

Go straight on.

Follow the road round to the left/right.

19

Lerntipp

Ein Vokabelheft anlegen

Ein Vokabelheft kostet normalerweise nur 1–2 Euro. Der Test auf dieser Seite zeigt Ihnen, wie Sie ein Vokabelheft oder einfach ein Blatt Papier als Lernhilfe gestalten können. Wenn Sie eine Seite angelegt haben, dann können Sie sich testen, indem Sie jeweils eine Spalte mit der Hand abdecken.

Test

Übertragen Sie die Vorlage auf ein Blatt Papier und vervollständigen Sie die Einträge (1–14).

page	Translations	Flug
6	f...[1]	jdn. a...[2]
7	pick s.b. up	Abteilung
8	d...[3]	M...[4]?
8	Would you like ...?	Lieferung
14	d...[5]	A...[6]
19	traffic light	
	Definitions	the person who ...[7]
6	boss	the department which ...[8]
10	IT	
	False friends	Warenhaus (English: department store)
10	warehouse (German: Lagergebäude)	Flur (English: corridor)
13	f...[9] (German: Etage, Boden)	
	Synonyms	receive
10	g...[10]	r...[11]
13	correct	
	Opposites	left
9	r...[12]	e...[13]
11	entrance	Mr
12	M...[14] (sometimes Mrs)	

Lust auf mehr Vokabeltraining?
Dann schnell auf die Website
Cornelsen.de und folgenden
Webcode eingeben: **JBvocab1**

Rezeption: Hörverstehen

ALLGEMEINE INFORMATIONEN ZUM PRÜFUNGSTEIL

Dieser Teil der Prüfung kommt am Anfang und macht 20 % der Punktwerte der schriftlichen Prüfung aus. Als Prüfling hören Sie eine berufsbezogene Nachricht, aus der Sie Informationen entnehmen und üblicherweise in ein Formular (z. B. ein Memo) auf Deutsch eintragen. Vor dem Hören dürfen Sie die Aufgabe durchlesen. Es ist empfehlenswert, während des Zuhörens Notizen zu machen und danach die Antworten binnen zehn Minuten zu notieren, damit Ihnen ausreichend Zeit für den Rest der Prüfung bleibt. Auf dieser Seite finden Sie zwei Aufgaben dieses Typs.

1

1/12

Ihre Firma Mainhattan Fairs & Events betreut viele ausländische Firmen, die in Frankfurt auf den Messen als Aussteller teilnehmen. Heute ruft eine potenzielle Kundin an. Da Sie gerade nicht in Ihrem Büro sind, hat die Kundin eine Nachricht auf Ihrem Anrufbeantworter hinterlassen.

- Sie hören die Nachricht zwei Mal.

- Vor dem Hören lesen Sie bitte, welche Informationen Sie in dem Formular auf Deutsch erfassen sollen.

MAINHATTAN
Fairs & Events

1 Name des Anrufers: ...

2 Woher kommt der Anrufer? ...

3 Telefonnummer – geschäftlich: ...

4 Telefonnummer – mobil: ...

5 Wann ist der Anrufer zu erreichen? ...

6 Welchen Zeitunterschied gibt es zwischen Singapur und Deutschland? ...

7 Was möchte der Anrufer in Frankfurt tun? ...

8 Wann sollten Sie besser nicht anrufen? ...

2

1/13

Sie arbeiten in einer Firma, die häufig Geschäfte in England tätigt. Heute fliegen Sie nach London und von dort fahren Sie mit dem Zug weiter zu Ihrem Kunden nach York. Ihr Kollege fährt nach King's Lynn. Sie stehen jetzt am Bahnsteig im Londoner Bahnhof King's Cross und hören einige Ansagen.

- Beantworten Sie die nachfolgenden Fragen auf Deutsch. Sie hören die Ansagen zwei Mal.

- Lesen Sie sich vor dem Hören die Fragen durch.

1 Welche Nummer hat der Zug, der nach York fährt?
2 Auf welchem Bahngleis müssen Sie in den Zug nach York einsteigen?
3 Wann fährt der Zug nach York heute los?
4 Wie viel Verspätung hat der Zug heute?
5 Fährt der Zug nach King's Lynn heute pünktlich?
6 Wann ist die Abfahrtszeit des Zuges nach King's Lynn?
7 An welchem Gleis muss man heute in den Zug einsteigen, wenn man nach King's Lynn fahren will?

Answering and transferring calls
Anrufe entgegennehmen und weiterleiten

THE SITUATION Ulla Brandt often receives calls in English, and she sometimes has to transfer these calls to other people.

1 | Answering a call

A Ordnen Sie die Begriffe (a–f) den englischen Bezeichnungen auf dem Telefon zu.

a aufnehmen
b externer Anruf
c interner Anruf
d halten
e Mailbox
f weiterleiten

voicemail

record
internal call
external call
hold
transfer

1/14

B Hören Sie das Telefongespräch zwischen Ulla und einem Kunden und beantworten Sie die Fragen auf Deutsch.

1 Für welche Art von Firma arbeitet der Anrufer?
2 Ist es eine deutsche Firma?
3 Von wo aus ruft er an?
4 Was tut er dort?
5 Weshalb ruft er an?
6 Wen will er sprechen?
7 In welcher Abteilung arbeitet die Person, mit der er sprechen will?

C Hören Sie noch einmal zu und beantworten Sie die Fragen. Benutzen Sie die ‚Useful language'-Box als Hilfe.

1 Wie können Sie nach dem Namen des Anrufers fragen?
2 Was können Sie sagen, wenn Sie Hilfe anbieten möchten?
3 Wie können Sie jemanden bitten, etwas für Sie zu buchstabieren?
4 Was können Sie sagen, wenn Sie prüfen wollen, ob Sie einen Buchstaben richtig verstanden haben?

USEFUL LANGUAGE	
How can I help you?	Wie kann ich Ihnen helfen?
Please go ahead.	Bitte fahren Sie fort.
What's your name, please?	Wie ist bitte Ihr Name?
Could you spell that, please?	Könnten Sie das bitte buchstabieren?
Sorry. Is that … for …?	Entschuldigung. Ist das … für …?
You need to talk to … in …	Sie müssen mit … in … sprechen.

2 | Spelling on the phone

A   Lesen Sie die Info über das Buchstabieren am Telefon. Arbeiten Sie dann mit einem Partner und buchstabieren Sie sich gegenseitig Ihre Namen.

Buchstabieren

- Namen oder andere Wörter mit schwieriger Schreibweise sollten immer buchstabiert werden. Damit andere das gut verstehen können, ist es nützlich, das internationale Buchstabieralphabet zu benutzen. Man sagt dann z. B. *A for Alpha, B for Bravo.*

A	Alpha	**H**	Hotel	**O**	Oscar	**V**	Victor
B	Bravo	**I**	India	**P**	Papa	**W**	Whisky
C	Charlie	**J**	Juliette	**Q**	Quebec	**X**	X-Ray
D	Delta	**K**	Kilo	**R**	Romeo	**Y**	Yankee
E	Echo	**L**	Lima	**S**	Sierra	**Z**	Zulu
F	Foxtrot	**M**	Mike	**T**	Tango		
G	Golf	**N**	November	**U**	Uniform		

- Wenn zwei Buchstaben hintereinander gleich sind, können Sie z. B. *double B* sagen.
- Achten Sie auf die unterschiedliche Aussprache von Z im britischen und im amerikanischen Englisch: BE: *zed*; AE: *zee.*

1/15

B   Hören Sie die Nachrichten auf einem Anrufbeantworter und notieren Sie die Namen der Personen, die angerufen haben.

C   Partnerarbeit: Wechseln Sie sich beim Buchstabieren und Aufschreiben der folgenden Namen ab.

Partner A
- Ms Aznar
- Mrs Dassault
- Dr Weever
- Mr Priandello

Partner B
- Mr Suarez
- Mrs Vanwatt
- Ms Bannard
- Dr Andropov

3 | Transferring a call

1/16

Lesen Sie die Ausdrücke (a–e). Hören Sie sich dann das Telefongespräch an und notieren Sie die Reihenfolge, in der die Ausdrücke verwendet werden.

a   'You're welcome.'
b   'I'll put you through to Mr Bach now.'
c   'I'll transfer you now, Mr Ravel.'
d   'Could you hold the line for a moment?'
e   'I'll try another number for you.'

4 | Role-playing a phone call

Partnerarbeit: Führen Sie ein Telefonat auf Englisch an Ihrem Arbeitsplatz als Rollenspiel durch. Einer von Ihnen ist der Angestellte, der andere ist der Anrufer. Einigen Sie sich zuerst darauf, worum es in dem Anruf gehen soll. Partner A verwendet File 3 auf S. 136, Partner B verwendet File 7 auf S. 137.

THE SITUATION • **Mr Schlegel, the manager of Restaurant Seeblick, is out. Meike Krenz answers the phone for him.**

1 Taking a message

1/17

A Hören Sie das Telefongespräch und vervollständigen Sie Meikes teilweise schon geschriebene Nachricht.

B Hören Sie das Gespräch noch einmal und notieren Sie die Ausdrücke, die Meike für Folgendes benutzt. Verwenden Sie die ‚Useful language'–Box als Hilfe.

> *Telefonnotiz*
> *Für:*   *Herrn Schlegel*
> *Von:*   *...*
> *Betreff:*   *Anfrage für Geschäftsessen*
> *Nachricht: Herr Navarro möchte wissen, ob wir ... können.*

1 Asking for the caller's message
2 Asking the caller to spell his name
3 Offering to take a message
4 Asking for the caller's name

2 Understanding dates and numbers

1/18

A Hören Sie den weiteren Verlauf des Gesprächs zwischen Meike und Herrn Navarro und vervollständigen Sie den zweiten Teil der Nachricht.

> *Das Geschäftsessen ist für ... Personen am ... Dezember.*
> *Bitte rufen Sie Herrn Navarro so bald wie möglich zurück.*
> *Tel. Büro: ... Handy: ...*

USEFUL LANGUAGE		
Can I take a message?	*Kann ich eine Nachricht aufnehmen?*
Could I have your name, please?	*Wie lautet Ihr Name, bitte?*
Could you spell that, please?	*Könnten Sie das bitte buchstabieren?*
What's the message, please?	*Wie lautet Ihre Nachricht?*
Let me read that back to you: ...	*Ich wiederhole: ...*
... will call you back as soon as possible.	*... wird Sie baldmöglichst zurückrufen.*
You're very welcome.	*Sehr gern geschehen.*

B Lesen Sie die Info über Datumsangaben und Telefonnummern. Nennen Sie die Punkte, die in dem Gespräch zwischen Meike und Herrn Navarro vorkommen. Hören Sie das Gespräch bei Bedarf noch einmal.

Datumsangaben und Telefonnummern

- Sie können das Datum unterschiedlich ausdrücken, z. B. *the 15th of May / May the 15th / May 15th / May 15*. Schreiben Sie das Datum so: *15th / 15 May* oder *May 15th / 15*.
- Wenn zwei aufeinanderfolgende Zahlen gleich sind, können Sie z. B. *double 4* sagen.
- Die Zahl 0 können Sie entweder *oh* oder *zero* nennen.
- Verwechseln Sie nicht *teens* (z. B. 13, 14) mit *tens* (z. B. 30, 40).
- Fassen Sie Zahlenpaare nicht zusammen; sagen Sie z. B. *four-two-five-nine* (nicht *forty-two, fifty-nine*).
- Bei internationalen Telefonnummern beginnen Sie mit *plus, zero-zero, double zero* oder *double oh*, dann nennen Sie die Landesvorwahl und den Rest der Nummer (ohne die Null aus der Vorwahl). Sie können z. B. schreiben +49 (0)711 244238, und Sie können sagen *plus-4-9-7-double 1-2-double 4-2-3-8*.

1/19

C Hören Sie zu und notieren Sie die Zahlen, die die Anrufer auf Ihrem Anrufbeantworter hinterlassen haben.

1 Telefonnummer im Büro
2 Handynummer
3 Datum
4 Mengen
5 Auftragsnummern

D Partner A benutzt File 4 auf S. 136, Partner B benutzt File 8 auf S. 137. Wechseln Sie sich ab – einer liest die Sätze vor, der andere schreibt die Zahlen und Daten auf, die er hört.

3 | Taking and leaving messages

★ **A** Partnerarbeit: Nehmen Sie die Rollen von Herrn Schlegel und von Herrn Navarros Assistentin, Maria Gomez, ein. Herrn Schlegel liegen jetzt Meikes Notizen aus 1A und 2A vor, und er ruft zurück, um zu sagen, dass sie das Geschäftsessen für 50 Personen am 13. Dezember ausrichten können. Maria nimmt die Nachricht entgegen. Verwenden Sie die ‚Useful language'-Box auf S. 24 als Hilfe.

★★ **B** Wechseln Sie sich mit einem Partner ab, Anrufe an Ihrem Arbeitsplatz zu tätigen und entgegenzunehmen. Bevor Sie anfangen, notieren Sie sich bitte:

- den Name einer Person, die Sie erreichen wollen;
- eine kurze Nachricht, die eine Nummer und ein Datum enthält;
- eine Telefonnummer für den Rückruf.

Zeigen Sie das nicht Ihrem Partner, bevor das Gespräch beendet ist. Vergleichen Sie erst dann die Notizen und die Ergebnisse. Die Details sollten übereinstimmen!

x

THE SITUATION | Katja Sommerfeldt is a trainee at a shop called **Sea Star Sport** which sells water sports equipment. Her colleague **Florian Hahn** has gone out, and he has left her a memo.

1 Calling a company

A   Lesen Sie Florians Notiz und sagen Sie mit eigenen Worten, was Katja tun soll.

> Hallo Katja,
>
> ich habe viel Gutes über einen italienischen Lieferanten gehört: SurfCity in Sorrento. Bitte ruf dort an unter +39 73 811698 und bitte sie, uns die technischen Daten und eine Preisliste für ihre neuen Surfbretter zu mailen.
>
> Frag nach Carlo Romano: Mit ihm habe ich bei der Aqua Sport-Messe letzten Monat gesprochen.
>
> Ich brauche die Unterlagen morgen früh auf meinem Schreibtisch.
>
> Danke.
>
> Florian

SurfCity

Our new Storm Force range

B   Ordnen Sie den englischen Ausdrücken (1–4) die entsprechenden deutschen Ausdrücke aus Florians Notiz zu.

1   technical specifications   **3**   price list
2   trade fair   **4**   supplier

1/20

C   Hören Sie zu und notieren Sie, wann Carlo Romano wieder im Büro sein wird, und schreiben Sie die Handynummer auf, die Katja bekommt.

D   Hören Sie noch einmal zu und beantworten Sie die Fragen.

1   What can you say to move the conversation into English?
2   How can you say where you are calling from?
3   How can you ask to speak to someone?
4   What can you say to find out when someone will return?
5   How can you show that you plan to make a note of something?

USEFUL LANGUAGE

Questions	Answers
I'm sorry, but can we speak English?	I'm calling from …, in …
How can I help you?	I'd like to speak to …, please.
When will … be back?	Let me make a note of that.
Would you like to try his mobile number?	Let me read that back to you: …

2   When communicating is difficult

1/21

A   Katja ruft Herrn Romano auf seinem Handy an. Hören Sie zu und notieren Sie, wann die beiden wieder miteinander sprechen werden.

B   Hören Sie das Gespräch noch einmal und schreiben Sie die englischen Ausdrücke auf, die den folgenden deutschen Ausdrücken (1–4) entsprechen.

     1   ‚Entschuldigung, das habe ich nicht verstanden.'
     2   ‚Ich verstehe Sie leider nur sehr abgehackt.'
     3   ‚Der Empfang ist hier nicht sehr gut.'
     4   ‚Entschuldigung, könnten Sie etwas lauter sprechen?'

3   Getting through

A   Schauen Sie sich die Info über E-Mail-Adressen an. Lesen Sie das Beispiel laut vor.

.	dot	**co/com**	co/com (= company)
@	at	**org**	org (= organization)
_	underscore	**de/uk**	d-e (= Germany) / u-k (= United Kingdom)
lower case		**UPPER CASE / CAPITAL**	
Example:	Write:	Romano.c@surf_city.co.it	
	Say:	capital R-o-m-a-n-o-dot-c-at-s-u-r-f-underscore-c-i-t-y-dot-co-dot-i-t	

B   Hören Sie sich das Telefongespräch an und notieren Sie Katjas E-Mail-Adresse.

1/22

C   Partner A verwendet File 10 auf S. 138, Partner B verwendet File 13 auf S. 139. Wechseln Sie sich mit dem Vorlesen und Aufschreiben der E-Mail-Adressen ab.

D   Partnerarbeit: Partner B muss eine Firma im Ausland anrufen, Partner A nimmt die Rolle seiner Kontaktperson ein. Klären Sie zuerst, mit welcher Firma und welcher Person Sie sprechen wollen sowie welche Information Sie benötigen (z. B. Preisliste). Führen Sie dann das Rollenspiel auf Englisch durch und wechseln Sie anschließend die Rollen.

Partner A

Melden Sie sich mit dem Firmennamen.

Partner B

Stellen Sie sich und Ihre Firma vor.
Fragen Sie nach einer bestimmten Person.

Sie sind der richtige Ansprechpartner.
Fragen Sie, wie Sie helfen können.

Erklären Sie Ihr Anliegen und bitten Sie um Zusendung der Infos per E-Mail.

Fragen Sie nach der E-Mail-Adresse.

Nennen Sie Ihre E-Mail-Adresse.

Prüfen Sie, ob Sie sie richtig notiert haben.

Bestätigen oder korrigieren Sie die Adresse.

Versprechen Sie, heute die Infos zu schicken.

Bedanken und verabschieden Sie sich.

(**THE SITUATION**) You need a business card in English. You have found four nice business cards from England to use as models.

1 Understanding business cards

Lesen Sie die Visitenkarten und beantworten Sie die folgenden Fragen.
Mehrere Antworten können möglich sein.

1   Who can you contact when you need a place to spend the night in London?
2   Who can you contact when your office is too hot in the summer?
3   Who can you contact anytime?
4   Who can you find in old people's flats?
5   Who travels around?
6   Whose card tells us that he/she has a special qualification?
7   Who doesn't work with the public?
8   Who works with other businesses?
9   Who works in a team?
10 Who wears special clothes to work?

> **REMEMBER**
>
> I work
> he/she work<u>s</u>

air conditioning   Klimaanlage
certified   (staatlich usw.) geprüft
elderly   Senioren
laboratory   Labor

Thomas Smith
Home care for the elderly

Emergency telephone number
020 2463 7465

www.carer4hire.co.uk

Ian Robinson
Certified technician

 Maxxx
Air Conditioning
Repair Service

43 Blackwell Lane
London, SW3 5RG

Tel: 020 56475947
E-mail: ian.robinson@maxxxair.co.uk

 Rex Laboratories

Mindy Logan
Laboratory Assistant

131 Canal Street, Manchester, M4 4FS
www.rexlaboratories.co.uk
E-mail: info@rexlaboratories.co.uk

🏠 HOTEL BUCKINGHAM

Anita Hemingway

76 Oxford Street, London, NW1 7SE
Tel: 020 9867 4536
E-mail: bookings@hotelbuckingham.co.uk
Web: www.hotelbuckingham.co.uk

2 | Designing a business card

A Eine gute Visitenkarte enthält maximal sechs verschiedene Informationen. Erstellen Sie eine Liste mit sechs Angaben für die Gestaltung Ihrer eigenen Visitenkarte.

> person's name • job title • (emergency) phone number • company name • company industry
> fax number • e-mail address • website address • address • photo • company logo
> bank account details

B Gestalten Sie mit den sechs Informationen aus Aufgabe 2A Ihre Visitenkarte. Verwenden Sie die Beispiele aus Aufgabe 1 als Hilfe. Sie können viele Berufsbezeichnungen auf S. 160 finden.

(NEW SITUATION) You meet a new business associate.

3 | Introducing yourself and explaining your work

★ **A** Verwenden Sie die ‚Useful language'-Box, um fünf Sätze zu schreiben, die Ihren Beruf charakterisieren.

★★ **B** Tauschen Sie mit einem Partner Visitenkarten aus. Stellen Sie sich vor und beschreiben Sie Ihren Beruf. Benutzen Sie dazu Ausdrücke aus der ‚Useful language'-Box. Sprechen Sie mindestens eine Minute lang.

✈ **C** Notieren Sie noch mehr Sätze über Ihren Beruf. Tauschen Sie mit einem anderen Partner Visitenkarten aus und sprechen Sie noch einmal über Ihren Beruf.

USEFUL LANGUAGE	
Contact me when you need …	Kontaktieren Sie mich, wenn Sie … brauchen.
You can contact me …	Sie können mich …
on weekdays from 9 a.m. to 5 p.m.	werktags zwischen 9:00 und 17:00 Uhr kontaktieren.
anytime.	jederzeit kontaktieren.
You can find me …	Sie können mich …
in my office. / in my workshop.	in meinem Büro. / meiner Werkstatt antreffen.
I travel around.	Ich reise herum.
I have …	Ich habe …
training in …	eine (Fach-)Ausbildung im Bereich …
a special qualification in …	eine spezielle Qualifikation im Bereich …
I work …	Ich arbeite …
with the public. / with customers.	mit der Öffentlichkeit. / mit Kunden.
with other businesses.	mit anderen Unternehmen.
alone. / in a team.	alleine. / in einem Team.
I wear …	Ich trage …
a uniform. / special clothes.	eine Uniform. / spezielle Kleidung.
my own clothes.	meine eigene Kleidung.

> **THE SITUATION** **You and some friends are looking for jobs outside of Germany.**

1 Understanding job adverts

Lesen Sie die drei Stellenanzeigen und die Profile der vier Jobsuchenden (*job-seekers*). Ordnen Sie jeden Job einem Bewerber zu. Einer der Vier ist für keine der Stellen geeignet.

Job-seeker 1
Thomas Bergmann
- worked as a mechanic for a car manufacturer
- repairs machines
- likes working outdoors

Job-seeker 2
Mehmet Hason
- looking for a summer job
- qualification in gastronomy from vocational school
- likes working with people
- no working experience

WANTED – Administrative Assistant. You will work as an administrative assistant at a car manufacturer. You will answer the telephone and work in a team. You must work independently. You must have commitment to the job. Experience wanted. No qualifications necessary. <u>Click here</u> to apply.

Wind Turbine Technician
- Repair broken machines
- Help in all areas of maintenance
- Give safety recommendations

Job requirements
The successful candidate will have technical training. Must have a driving licence. Must be a leader and hard-working. Must be able to travel for long periods of time.

Send CV and cover letter to JMB Turbines, 1232 Springfield Road, Albany, NY, 12256-8558.

Waiter/Waitress
The Windy Breeze Restaurant is looking for a waiter or waitress. No experience necessary, but must have an outgoing personality. Must be flexible, willing to work long hours, evenings and weekends, from June to August. You must always be friendly to guests. Salary is minimum wage plus tips. Call Gary on 020 2846 8362.

administrative assistant	Sekretär/in
necessary	nötig
maintenance	Instandhaltung
recommendation	Empfehlung
outgoing personality	aufgeschlossene Persönlichkeit
minimum wage	Mindestlohn
tip	Trinkgeld

Job-seeker 3
Annika Schlaich
· has eight years'
  restaurant and café
  experience
· can only work part-
  time
· wants to work
  from home

Job-seeker 4
Anh Le
· qualification in
  office
  administration from
  vocational school
· was an intern at an
  office for one
  month

2 | Talking about yourself and your job

1/23

A Hören Sie sich an, wie Angela und Greg über ihre Jobs sprechen. Wer von beiden
arbeitet als Kellner/in und wer als Sekretär/in?

B Sind die folgenden Aussagen richtig oder falsch? Begründen Sie Ihre
Antworten auf Deutsch.

  KMK

    1   Greg hasst seinen Job.
    2   Angela hat eine aufgeschlossene Persönlichkeit.
    3   Angela mag alle Gäste im Restaurant.
    4   Greg möchte Automechaniker werden.
    5   Greg telefoniert gerne.
    6   Angela denkt, dass Greg in seinem Job bleiben sollte.

C Hören Sie den Dialog noch einmal und machen Sie eine Liste mit allen beruflichen
Anforderungen, die von Angela und Greg erwähnt werden.

D Unterstreichen Sie die beiden Anforderungen, die für Sie in Ihrem Berufsleben am
wichtigsten sein werden, und begründen Sie Ihre Wahl.

E Schreiben Sie fünf Sätze über Ihren Job oder einen Job, den Sie gerne hätten.
Verwenden Sie Ausdrücke aus den Stellenanzeigen, der Hörübung und der ‚Useful
language'-Box.

F Berichten Sie einem Partner, welche Eigenschaften für Ihren Job wichtig sind.
Sprechen Sie mindestens eine Minute. Verwenden Sie Ausdrücke aus den
Stellenanzeigen, der Hörübung und der ‚Useful language'-Box.

USEFUL LANGUAGE			
	You must have …	a qualification in … an outgoing personality	commitment to the job initiative
	You must be …	friendly independent creative able to work in a team	flexible a leader a good communicator hard-working

THE SITUATION You and two of your friends are applying for jobs and internships outside of Germany.

1 Your friends' experience

A Lesen Sie die zwei folgenden Lebensläufe. Diskutieren Sie mit einem Partner, für welche Jobs die beiden Personen geeignet sein könnten.

Name: Sarah Nell

2015	Driving licence and first aid certificate
2013 – present	Apprenticeship in hairdressing at Haireinspaziert; Willy-Brandt-Berufsschule (vocational school), Mannheim
2007 – 2013	Adam-Langhans-Realschule, Heidelberg; 10th grade school leaving certificate
2013	Two weeks' work experience, Titanic Reisen, Heidelberg
2011 – 2013	Newspaper delivery, Heidelberg

Name: Christian Möller

2016	KMK Foreign Language Certificate, English, Level I (A2)
2015 – present	Berufsbildende Schule Technik (vocational school), Braunschweig
2016	Programmed iPhone app 'Bullet Train' – won 'Best New App' award from appswelike.de
2015	Designed Photoshots website
2010 – 2015	Hauptschule Boschstraße, Braunschweig; 9th grade school leaving certificate

1/24

B Hören Sie, wie Sarah und Christian über ihre Erfahrungen sprechen. Beide vergessen jeweils einen Punkt aus ihren Lebensläufen zu erwähnen – welchen?

C Das Diagramm auf S. 33 zeigt die englischen Bezeichnungen für die deutschen Schulformen. Bitte beachten Sie aber, dass es nicht immer eine direkte Entsprechung im Englischen gibt. Vervollständigen Sie die unten dargestellte Schullaufbahn von Sarah und Christian.

Sarah:	primary school	→	?	→	?
Christian:	primary school	→	?	→	?

primary school	secondary school		higher education
	Hauptschule*	vocational school	vocational college
	Realschule	vocational school with apprenticeship (dual system)	vocational academy
	Gymnasium		university
	comprehensive school	vocational college	

* Hauptschule, Realschule und Gymnasium werden manchmal als *secondary modern school, higher secondary modern school* und *grammar school* übersetzt.

2 | Your own education and experience

A Zeichnen Sie Ihre eigene Schullaufbahn in gleicher Weise auf wie für Sarah und Christian in Übung 1C.

B Legen Sie auf einem separaten Blatt Papier eine Liste mit Ihren eigenen Qualifikationen und Erfahrungen an. Erfassen Sie alles seit Ihrem 11. Lebensjahr, z. B. Schulen, Auszeichnungen und spezielle Kurse, Ferienjobs und freiwillige Arbeit.

C Sprechen Sie mit einem Partner über Ihre Qualifikationen und Erfahrungen. Verwenden Sie Ihre Notizen aus Übung 2B und die Ausdrücke aus der ‚Useful language'-Box.

REMEMBER

I've = I have
I've worked/gone/done
Where have you worked/
   gone/done … ?

I have a …
Do you have a … ?
What … do you have?

USEFUL LANGUAGE

9th grade school leaving certificate	*Hauptschulabschluss*
10th grade school leaving certificate	*Realschulabschluss / mittlere Reife*
What experience do you have?	*Welche Erfahrungen hast du / haben Sie?*
What school leaving certificate do you have?	*Welchen Schulabschluss hast du / haben Sie?*
I've done an apprenticeship at …	*Ich habe eine Ausbildung bei … gemacht.*
I've had a summer job as a/an …	*Ich hatte einen Ferienjob als …*
I've volunteered as a/an …	*Ich habe freiwillig als … gearbeitet.*
I have an award for …	*Ich habe eine Auszeichnung für …*
I have a driving licence.	*Ich habe einen Führerschein.*
I have work experience in …	*Ich habe Berufserfahrung als …*

CULTURE

Schulsysteme sind in jedem Land unterschiedlich. Daher sind einige deutsche Bezeichnungen, wie ‚Hauptschule', schwierig zu übersetzen.

Im Vereinigten Königreich (England, Nordirland, Schottland und Wales) gehen die Kinder vom 5. bis zum 11. Lebensjahr zur *primary school* und zwischen dem 11. und 18. Lebensjahr zur *secondary school*. In den USA gehen die Kinder zwischen 6 und 11 Jahren zur *primary school*, zwischen 11 und 14 zur *middle school* und zwischen 14 und 18 zur *high school*.

Wenn Sie mit Menschen aus anderen Ländern über Ihre Schullaufbahn sprechen, ist es manchmal einfacher, nicht von ‚Klassen', sondern von ‚Altersstufen' zu sprechen.

THE SITUATION You and your Scottish colleague Melissa Johnston must travel to Barcelona for a meeting with Pablo Flores from the Spanish branch of your company.

1 Understanding small talk

1/25

A Hören Sie den ersten Teil eines Gesprächs, in dem Melissa und Pablo über das Wetter und über Sport reden. Beantworten Sie die Fragen.

1 What does Pablo say about the weather later today?
2 What does Melissa want to do this afternoon?
3 What will Melissa do tomorrow?
4 What football team does Melissa support?
5 What is Pablo's favourite sport?

1/25–26

B Hören Sie jetzt das ganze Gespräch. Schreiben Sie so viele Ausdrücke wie möglich auf, die Pablo und Melissa verwenden, um das Wetter und ihr Interesse für bestimmte Sportarten zu beschreiben. Vergleichen Sie Ihre Antworten mit anderen, um die Ausdrücke zu finden, die Ihnen noch fehlen.

competition	Wettkampf
degree	Grad
support	unterstützen

2 Talking about the weather

A Schauen Sie sich die Wettersymbole an. Ordnen Sie die Wörter in der Box den passenden Symbolen (1–6) zu.

> cloudy • rain • snow • sunny • thunderstorm • windy

1   2   3   4   5   6

B Unterhalten Sie sich mit einem Partner über das Wetter in Ihrer Region zu verschiedenen Jahreszeiten. Benutzen Sie die Ausdrücke, die Sie in 1B aufgeschrieben haben und die ‚Useful language'-Box als Hilfe.

USEFUL LANGUAGE

Tomorrow the weather will be sunny/cloudy/clear.	Morgen wird das Wetter sonnig/bewölkt/klar.
Spring/autumn is mild/wet/windy.	Der Frühling/Herbst ist mild/nass/windig.
In our region it rains a lot in summer / usually snows in winter.	In unserer Region regnet es im Sommer viel / schneit es im Winter normalerweise.
I support …	Ich unterstütze / bin ein Fan von …
My favourite player/team is …	Mein Lieblingsspieler/Lieblingsteam ist …

C Lesen Sie den Wetterbericht für Barcelona und machen Sie eine Wettervorhersage. Benutzen Sie als Hilfe die ‚Useful language'-Box.

> **REMEMBER**
>
> It **will rain** tomorrow.
> The weather **won't be** sunny on Tuesday.

Thursday	Friday	Saturday	Sunday	Monday	Tuesday
Sunny	Sunny	Showers	Sunny	Mostly sunny	Windy
12° High 8° Low	17° High 4° Low	8° High 3° Low	10° High 6° Low	11° High 8° Low	9° High 5° Low
Chance of rain: 0%	Chance of rain: 0%	Chance of rain: 70%	Chance of rain: 0%	Chance of rain: 10%	Chance of rain: 15%

3 | Talking about sports

A Arbeiten Sie in Gruppen und schreiben Sie alle Ihnen bekannten englischen Bezeichnungen für Sportarten auf. Stellen Sie Ihre Liste der Klasse vor und sagen Sie, welche Sportarten die Mitglieder Ihrer Gruppe am meisten mögen.

B Sprechen Sie mit einem Partner über Ihren Lieblingssport. Verwenden Sie dazu die folgenden Vorgaben.

Partner A

Partner B

What's your favourite sport?

My favourite sport is … . What about you?

I like … . Do you have a favourite player/team?

Yes, my favourite player/team is … What about you?

My favourite player/team is …

Do you often go to see … play?

Yes, I often … . / No, I never … . What about you?

Yes, I often … / No, I never …

✈ C Was können Sie noch über Ihren Lieblingssport sagen? Erzählen Sie es Ihrem Partner.

D Machen Sie Small Talk und stellen Sie Ihrem Partner möglichst viele Fragen.

> **CULTURE**
>
> **Small Talk** ist ein Ritual, wie das Händeschütteln, und englische Muttersprachler fühlen sich unwohl, wenn Sie keinen Small Talk machen. Dabei handelt es sich nicht um vorgetäuschte Freundlichkeit, sondern um einen Teil der englischsprachigen Kultur. Small Talk kann aus einem Satz bestehen oder eine längere Unterhaltung sein – auf jeden Fall muss er gemacht werden.

THE SITUATION You are at a trade fair in Cologne with your boss, Karl Klein. It is your job to find new customers for the company Shop Top.

1 Talking to a potential customer

1/27

A Schauen Sie sich die beiden Fotos oben an. Wo könnten sich die Personen aufhalten? Worüber sprechen sie möglicherweise gerade?

B Hören Sie sich ein Gespräch auf der Messe in Köln an. Welches der beiden Fotos passt zu dem Gespräch? Was meinen Sie: Fühlt sich die Frau wohl oder unwohl?

C Hören Sie das Gespräch noch einmal und beantworten Sie die Fragen.

1 What is the woman's name?
2 What is the man's name?
3 Where does the man come from?
4 Which company does he work for?
5 How many questions does the woman ask?
6 How many questions does the man ask?

D Vergleichen Sie Ihre Antworten mit denen eines Partners. Was glauben Sie, warum die Frau plötzlich gegangen ist, als der Mann ihr das Formular geben wollte?

2 Understanding small talk

1/28

A Hören Sie ein weiteres Gespräch auf der Messe. Sagen Sie mit Ihren eigenen Worten, worüber sich die beiden unterhalten.

★

B Hören Sie das Gespräch noch einmal. Notieren Sie sich in Partnerarbeit, wie viele Fragen Karl und Anne stellen. Ein Partner hört Karl genau zu, der andere Anne.

★★

C Hören Sie das Gespräch noch einmal. Schreiben Sie alle Ausdrücke auf, mit denen das Folgende gesagt wird.

1 How to introduce yourself
2 How to ask a person where he or she is from
3 Making a polite comment about a person's home town
4 Asking how long a person is staying in the city
5 How to recommend a restaurant
6 How to arrange to meet a person later

3 | Making small talk

A   Wählen Sie zwei mögliche Themen für Small Talk aus und notieren Sie sich zu jedem Thema mindestens drei Fragen. Verwenden Sie die ‚Useful language'-Box als Hilfe.

Books	Films	Food	Hobbies	Hotels
• crime	• action	• meat	• cycling	• bed & breakfast
• thriller	• comedy	• pasta	• games	• low-budget
Music	**Restaurants**	**Sports**	**Weather**	**Work**
• hip hop	• Chinese	• football	• rainy	• company
• pop	• Italian	• swimming	• sunny	• factory

B   Machen Sie mit einem Partner Small Talk. Verwenden Sie dazu die folgenden Angaben und die Fragen, die Sie in 3A notiert haben.

Partner A   **Partner B**

Introduce yourself.

Introduce yourself.

Ask where your partner is from.

Say where you are from and ask the same question.

Say where you are from.

Make a comment about the town or city.

Agree, and then make a comment about your partner's town or city.

Ask a question about a small talk topic.

Answer the question and ask your partner the same question.

Answer the question.

Ask a question about a new topic.

C   Machen Sie einen Wettbewerb: Führen Sie so lange wie möglich Small Talk mit einem Partner. Sprechen Sie ohne Unterbrechung über alle Themen aus 3A. Wenn Sie eine Pause machen, die länger als zehn Sekunden dauert, scheiden Sie aus.

USEFUL LANGUAGE	Questions	Answers
	Hi, my name's … . What's yours?	Pleased to meet you, …
	What do you think of …?	I think …
	Where are you from?	I'm from …
	Do you like …?	I (don't really) like …
	What … do you prefer?	I prefer …
	What's your favourite …?	My favourite … is/are … . What about you?

Lerntipp

Vokabeln bildlich darstellen

Man lernt Vokabeln effektiver, wenn man sie in einen Zusammenhang bringt, z. B. durch bildliche Anordnung. Dies sind drei Möglichkeiten, Vokabeln bildlich darzustellen: Flussdiagramm (Test 1), Tabelle (Test 2) oder Mindmap (Test 3). Flussdiagramme stellen Prozesse dar. Tabellen bieten eine Möglichkeit, sich Wortfamilien, Synonyme und Antonyme einzuprägen. Mind Maps eignen sich gut für thematisch verwandte Wörter.

Test 1

Vervollständigen Sie das Telefongespräch.

mobile • message • possible • out • like • back

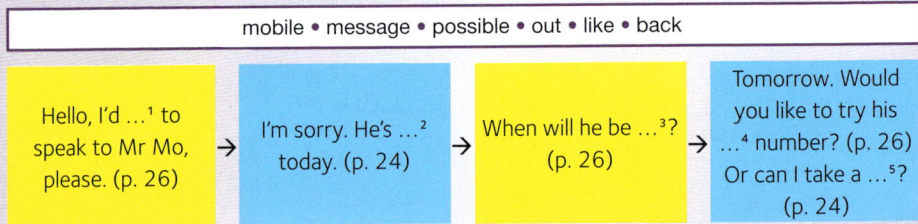

Hello, I'd …¹ to speak to Mr Mo, please. (p. 26) → I'm sorry. He's …² today. (p. 24) → When will he be …³? (p. 26) → Tomorrow. Would you like to try his …⁴ number? (p. 26) Or can I take a …⁵? (p. 24)

Test 2

Ergänzen Sie die unten stehende Tabelle mit Begriffen, die dasselbe oder das Gegenteil bedeuten, oder mit einem Wort aus derselben Wortfamilie.

English word	German word	word family	synonym	opposite
certified (p. 28)	(staatlich usw.) geprüft	noun: *certificate* (p. 32)		
weekdays (p. 29)	werktags			…¹ (p. 30)
recommend (p. 36)	empfehlen	noun: …² (p. 30)		
American high school (p. 33)	amerikanische Sekundarschule		British …³ school (p. 33)	
communicator (p. 31)	Kommunikator	verb: …⁴ (p. 27)		

Test 3

Übertragen Sie die unten stehende Mindmap auf ein Blatt Papier und ergänzen Sie sie mit den Begriffen, die Sie auf S. 34–35 gelernt haben.

clouds

sunshine

weather

WEB CODE Wollen Sie weiter mit visuellen Mitteln an Ihrem Wortschatz arbeiten? Dann gehen Sie auf Cornelsen.de und geben Sie folgenden Webcode ein: **JBvocab2**

Rezeption: Leseverstehen

ALLGEMEINE INFORMATIONEN ZUM PRÜFUNGSTEIL

In diesem Prüfungsteil können Sie 20 % der Punktwerte der schriftlichen Prüfung bekommen. Dazu müssen Sie zeigen, dass Sie den Inhalt eines berufsbezogenen, englischen Textes verstehen, indem Sie Fragen zum Text beantworten. Wenn Aussagen zum Text vorgegeben sind, müssen Sie entscheiden, ob die Aussagen richtig oder falsch sind und zudem Ihre Entscheidung begründen. Sie dürfen für die Bearbeitung ein zweisprachiges Wörterbuch benutzen – schlagen Sie jedoch nicht zu häufig nach, denn sonst verlieren Sie wertvolle Zeit. Nehmen Sie sich für diese Aufgabe etwa 15 Minuten Zeit.

Sie haben für Ihren Arbeitsplatz ein neues Telefon bekommen. Lesen Sie die Bedienungsanleitung. Entscheiden Sie, ob die Aussagen richtig oder falsch sind und begründen Sie Ihre Entscheidung auf Deutsch. Beantworten Sie die unten stehenden Fragen auf Deutsch.

How to use the telephone:

- For internal calls, pick up the receiver and dial the extension number.
- Dial '0' to make external calls.
- For calls within your country, dial '0' and then the number with the area code starting with '0'.
- For international calls, dial '0' and then the country code starting with '00'.

Basic functions:

- To put a call on hold, press the 'hold' button and put down the receiver.
- To return to a call on hold, press the 'hold' button and pick up the receiver.
- To transfer a call, press 'transfer', dial the recipient's extension and hang up the receiver.
- If a call is waiting on a colleague's line, the light next to their extension number will light up. To answer the call for another extension number, pick up the receiver and then press the 'on' button next to the red light.
- To forward calls, press the 'forward' button and dial the phone number you wish to forward the calls to. Then press 'OK'.
- To send calls to your voicemail, go to 'set up', select 'voicemail' and 'on'. Then press 'OK'.
- To save a message in your voicemail, select 'voicemail' and 'record message'. After saying your message, press 'save'.
- To hide your phone number when you make a call, press 'block' before you dial the number.

Aussagen		richtig	falsch
1	Für einen internen Anruf gibt man einfach die Durchwahlnummer ein. *Begründung: …*	…	…
2	Wird ein Anruf auf ‚warten‘ gestellt, dann kann er nicht mehr abgenommen werden. *Begründung: …*	…	…
3	Man kann eine Ansage aufnehmen. *Begründung: …*	…	…
4	Ihre Nummer wird immer auf dem Apparat der angerufenen Person angezeigt. *Begründung: …*	…	…
Fragen			
5	Sie müssen einen Anruf nach China tätigen. Die Telefonnummer ist +86 1 5678 8765. Wie lautet die komplette Nummer, die Sie wählen müssen?		
6	Ein Kunde hat Sie angerufen, aber er will Ihre Kollegin sprechen. Wie können Sie den Anruf weiterleiten?		
7	Sie müssen Ihr Büro für eine Stunde verlassen. Was können Sie tun, um Ihre Anrufe nicht zu verpassen? Nennen Sie zwei Möglichkeiten.		

THE SITUATION You are an assistant manager at AutoSales, a car sales company in Frankfurt. AutoSales sells cars and vans for work. Sometimes the company receives e-mails from customers in English, and it is your job to answer them.

1 Understanding customer enquiries

comfortable	bequem
fuel-efficient	Kraftstoff sparend
off-road	geländegängig
vehicle	Fahrzeug

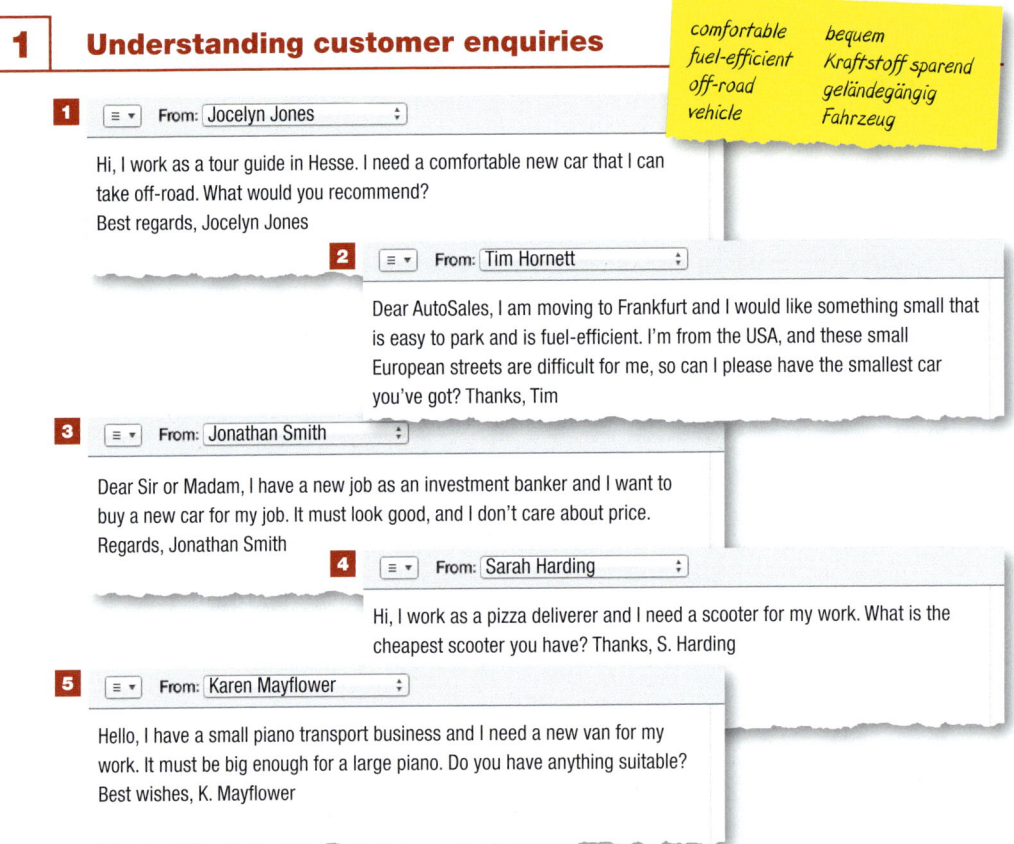

1 From: Jocelyn Jones

Hi, I work as a tour guide in Hesse. I need a comfortable new car that I can take off-road. What would you recommend?
Best regards, Jocelyn Jones

2 From: Tim Hornett

Dear AutoSales, I am moving to Frankfurt and I would like something small that is easy to park and is fuel-efficient. I'm from the USA, and these small European streets are difficult for me, so can I please have the smallest car you've got? Thanks, Tim

3 From: Jonathan Smith

Dear Sir or Madam, I have a new job as an investment banker and I want to buy a new car for my job. It must look good, and I don't care about price.
Regards, Jonathan Smith

4 From: Sarah Harding

Hi, I work as a pizza deliverer and I need a scooter for my work. What is the cheapest scooter you have? Thanks, S. Harding

5 From: Karen Mayflower

Hello, I have a small piano transport business and I need a new van for my work. It must be big enough for a large piano. Do you have anything suitable?
Best wishes, K. Mayflower

A Übertragen Sie die Tabelle unten auf ein Blatt Papier. Lesen Sie die E-Mails und tragen Sie die entsprechenden Informationen in Spalte B ein.

A. Name des Kunden	B. Wünsche des Kunden	C. Fahrzeug	D. Preis
1. Jocelyn Jones	…	…	…
2. Tim Hornett	…	…	…
3. Jonathan Smith	…	…	…
4. Sarah Harding	…	…	…
5. Karen Mayflower	…	…	…

B Lesen Sie nun die Beschreibungen von fünf verschiedenen Autos und vervollständigen Sie die Tabelle mit passenden Autos und den Preisangaben für jeden Kunden. Für einen der Kunden gibt es kein passendes Auto.

The Best of AutoSales

Car 1 – Bentley Continental Flying Spur

The most expensive car AutoSales has, the Bentley Continental Flying Spur is luxurious and comfortable.

Price: € 160,000

Car 2 – Mercedes Van

The Mercedes van can transport many things safely and easily, up to a weight of 3 tonnes.

Price: € 26,500

Car 3 – Smart Car

The Smart Car is one of the smallest cars in the world. Designed for the city, it is fuel-efficient, quiet, and easy to park!

Price: € 10,000

Car 4 – Range Rover

Perfect for off-road use, the Range Rover can handle any roads, even when there are no roads.

Price: € 75,000

Car 5 – Volkswagen Golf

The Volkswagen Golf is one of the most popular cars in Germany.

Price: € 14,800

> **USEFUL LANGUAGE**
>
> I would like to suggest …
> It is comfortable/
>   fuel-efficient/luxurious/
>   stylish/big.
> I'm afraid we do not have
>   a suitable vehicle for
>   you.
> The … costs …

2 | Replying to customer enquiries

A   Schreiben Sie einem der Kunden eine E-Mail und schlagen Sie ihm ein passendes Auto vor. Nennen Sie den Preis und die Gründe, warum das Auto für ihn geeignet ist.

B   Schreiben Sie eine E-Mail an den Kunden, für den Sie kein passendes Fahrzeug finden können. Entschuldigen Sie sich und schlagen Sie ihm eine Alternative aus Ihrem Bestand vor.

3 | Describing products

★★   A   Sie glauben, dass Sie in Ihrem jetzigen oder zukünftigen Job ein neues Auto benötigen. Beschreiben Sie das Fahrzeug für Ihren Chef, um ihn davon zu überzeugen, es für Sie anzuschaffen.

YOUR CHOICE

      For my job, I need a … because …

★   B   Beschreiben Sie ein Fahrzeug, das Sie gerne jetzt oder in Zukunft besitzen würden.

      I would like to drive a … because …

✈   C   Beschreiben Sie die Merkmale, die Ihr Wunschauto haben soll, in einer E-Mail-Anfrage an AutoSales.

THE SITUATION Björn is a retail assistant at The Media Shop. He works in the computer department. A customer wants to buy a new printer for the office.

Printers for the home and office

Mutama JQ120
Printer type: Inkjet
Print speed: 3.3 ppm
Paper capacity: 100 sheets
Connectivity: USB, Wi-Fi
Price: € 78
What Printer magazine rating ★★★★★

HC Inkster 2
Printer type: Inkjet
Print speed: 6 ppm B/W, 3 ppm Colour
Paper capacity: 60 sheets
Connectivity: USB
Price: € 55
What Printer magazine rating ★★★★★

Nikkoia L6680
Printer type: Laser B/W
Print speed: 19 ppm
Paper capacity: 160 sheets
Connectivity: USB, Wi-Fi
Price: € 120
What Printer magazine rating ★★★★★

PolarandPhotosnap
Printer type: Inkjet photo
Print speed: 1 ppm max.
Paper capacity: 10 sheets (4 cm x 6 cm)
Connectivity: USB, Bluetooth
Price: € 35
What Printer magazine rating ★★★★★

---

1 | Describing products

1/29

A Schauen Sie sich die Media Shop-Werbung für verschiedene Drucker an. Hören Sie dann, wie Björn mit einem Kunden spricht. Welchen Drucker beschreibt Björn?

B Beschreiben Sie in Partnerarbeit einander gegenseitig die anderen Drucker aus der Werbung. Verwenden Sie zur Orientierung das folgende Beispiel.

Example: The Mutama JQ120 is an inkjet printer.
It has a print speed of three-point-three pages per minute.
It has a paper capacity of 100 sheets.
It connects via USB and Wi-Fi.
The printer costs seventy-eight euros.

2 | Comparing products

Vergleichen Sie jetzt alle vier Drucker miteinander. Entscheiden Sie, welcher teurer/
günstiger/schneller etc. ist. Vergleichen Sie so viele unterschiedliche Eigenschaften
wie möglich. Verwenden Sie die ‚Useful language'-Box als Hilfe.

> **USEFUL LANGUAGE**
>
> The … is cheaper than the …
> The … is faster than the …
> The … is high quality and the … is low quality.
> The … has a bigger paper capacity than the …

> **REMEMBER**
>
> slow, slow**er**, slow**est**
> expensive, **more** expensive, **most** expensive

3 | Buying and selling products

Arbeiten Sie mit einem Partner. Einer spielt die Rolle des Verkäufers in The Media Shop,
der andere die des Kunden. Schauen Sie sich Ihre Rollenkarten an und führen Sie das
Gespräch.

Partner A: Kunde

Sie wollen einen Drucker für Ihr Büro
kaufen. Sie brauchen einen neuen
Farbdrucker und drucken täglich ungefähr
50 Seiten.

Sprechen Sie mit dem Verkäufer und
lassen Sie sich von ihm erklären, welcher
Drucker für Ihr Büro der beste ist.
Beantworten Sie die Fragen des
Verkäufers und stellen Sie die unten
aufgeführten Fragen.

Questions for the assistant

How much does it cost?
What's the print speed?

Partner B: Verkäufer

Stellen Sie die unten aufgeführten Fragen
und beantworten Sie die Fragen des
Kunden. Wählen Sie auf S. 42 den besten
Drucker für Ihren Kunden aus.

Questions for the customer

How many pages do you print each day?
Do you need colour or only black and white?

> **REMEMBER**
>
> Wenn es im Englischen um Zahlen geht, werden Punkt und Komma genau andersherum als im
> Deutschen verwendet.
>
> | Deutsch | Englisch |
> |---|---|
> | 1.004,05 m | 1,004.05 m *(one thousand and four point zero five metres)* |

THE SITUATION You are a sales assistant for Ergonomika GmbH. Ergonomika sells chairs for different purposes. Part of your job is presenting the product line to customers.

1 Saying where a product can be used

Arbeiten Sie mit einem Partner: Wählen Sie den passendsten Ort für jede der Sitzgelegenheiten.

This …

| 1 armchair | 2 bench | 3 dining chair | 4 office chair | 5 triple chair |

is perfect for …

a   a computer desk.
b   an expensive café.
c   a park.

d   a restaurant.
e   a waiting room.

2 Describing products

Finden Sie für jeden englischen Begriff die richtige Übersetzung. Verwenden Sie dann die Wörter, um Ihrem Partner jede der Sitzmöglichkeiten aus Übung 1 zu beschreiben.

1   adjustable height
2   back support
3   cheap
4   classic design
5   comfortable
6   long-lasting
7   stylish
8   swivel chair

a   bequem
b   Drehstuhl
c   klassisches Design
d   langlebig
e   preiswert
f   Rückenstütze
g   stillvoll/modisch
h   verstellbare Höhe

> This chair has a classic design.

> It's a swivel chair.

3 Presenting products

1/30

A   **Schauen Sie sich die Informationen zu den Stühlen auf S. 45 an und hören Sie, wie eine Verkäuferin sie präsentiert. Welche drei Stühle stellt sie vor?**

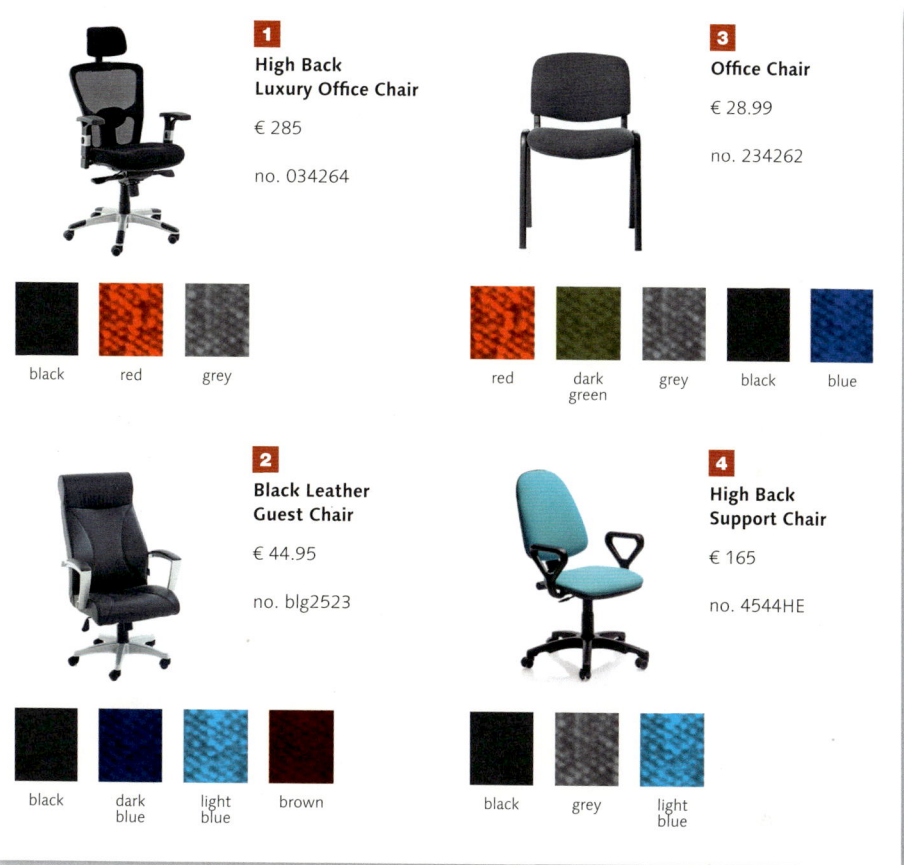

1
High Back
Luxury Office Chair

€ 285

no. 034264

black · red · grey

3
Office Chair

€ 28.99

no. 234262

red · dark green · grey · black · blue

2
Black Leather
Guest Chair

€ 44.95

no. blg2523

black · dark blue · light blue · brown

4
High Back
Support Chair

€ 165

no. 4544HE

black · grey · light blue

USEFUL LANGUAGE

It is stylish/cheap/long-lasting.
It's a swivel chair.
You can use it to …
It costs …
It has …
It is perfect for the CEO / the receptionist / people who sit for long hours.
It's made from …
It comes in black / grey / light blue / dark blue.

B Arbeiten Sie mit einem Partner und stellen Sie sich abwechselnd die Stühle aus 1 und 3A vor. Benutzen Sie dazu Ausdrücke aus der ‚Useful language'-Box.

★★ **C** Wählen Sie ein Produkt, das Ihre Firma oder eine Firma, die Sie kennen, herstellt. Notieren Sie sich die wichtigsten Produktmermale und beschreiben Sie das Produkt einem Partner. Verwenden Sie die ‚Useful language'-Box als Hilfe.

★ **D** Schauen Sie sich in Ihrem Klassenzimmer um und wählen Sie einen Stuhl, eine Tasche oder ein Kleidungsstück, das sich in Ihrer Nähe befindet. Beschreiben Sie einem Partner den Gegenstand so, als wäre er ein Produkt, das Sie ihm verkaufen wollen. Verwenden Sie die ‚Useful language'-Box als Hilfe.

YOUR CHOICE

THE SITUATION The coffee machine in your office does not work properly anymore. Your boss is angry – he wants his coffee!

1 Reading an instruction manual

A   Die Probleme mit der Kaffeemaschine sind, dass der Kaffee manchmal gar nicht herauskommt, und manchmal nur sehr langsam. Ihr Chef bittet Sie, einen Blick in die Bedienungsanleitung zu werfen und auf Deutsch einen Hinweiszettel zu erstellen. Der Zettel soll Ihre Kollegen darüber informieren, welche zwei Probleme auftreten können, warum sie auftreten und wie sie sie beheben können. **KMK**

filter
adjustment knob
spout

Problem	Cause	Solution
The coffee is not creamy.	The machine uses too little coffee.	Turn the adjustment knob to 3.
The coffee comes out of the machine too slowly.	The coffee is too fine.	Turn the adjustment knob to 5.
The coffee comes out of the machine too quickly.	The coffee is too coarse.	Turn the adjustment knob to 2.
The coffee does not come out.	The spout is blocked.	Scrape out the dry coffee.
The machine does not give out coffee, only water.	The filter is blocked.	Take out the coffee inside the filter, then clean the inside of the machine.
The machine does not work at all.	The machine is not plugged in.	Check that the power cable is plugged in.
If the coffee machine still does not work, please call our hotline on 0800 979 767.		

B   Schauen Sie sich die Bedienungsanleitung noch einmal an. Sprechen Sie mit einem Partner über mögliche Gründe für die nachfolgenden Probleme, und wie Sie diese lösen können.

1   The coffee is not creamy.
2   The coffee comes out too quickly.
3   The machine only gives out water.
4   The machine does not work.

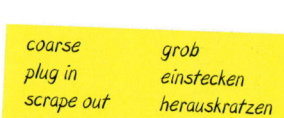

coarse — grob
plug in — einstecken
scrape out — herauskratzen

✈ C   Notieren Sie erklärende Hinweise und mögliche Lösungen auf Deutsch für die Probleme in 1B.

(NEW SITUATION) **Now the coffee machine doesn't work at all. Your boss asks you to call the hotline of the company who made the machine.**

2 | Calling a hotline

A   Tauschen Sie sich in Gruppen über Ihre Erfahrungen mit Hotlines aus und notieren Sie sich die wichtigsten Vor- und Nachteile.

B   Wenn Sie bei einer Hotline anrufen, sollten Sie sich kurzfassen. Notieren Sie mithilfe der ‚Useful language'-Box passende Antworten auf die folgenden Sätze.

1   'Hello, welcome to the Fando Electrical hotline. How may I help you?'
2   'What's the model number?'
3   'What exactly is wrong with it?'
4   'I think the spout is blocked. Have you scraped out the coffee?'
5   'Is the machine plugged in?'
6   'The spout is broken. Please e-mail the company and ask them to send you a new spout. Thank you and goodbye.'

C   Führen Sie das folgende Gespräch mit der Hotline von Fando Electrical in einem Rollenspiel mit einem Partner.

Partner A

Begrüßen Sie den Kunden und fragen Sie, was Sie für ihn tun können.

Partner B

Sagen Sie, dass Ihre Kaffeemaschine kaputt ist.

Fragen Sie, was genau damit nicht in Ordnung ist.

Sagen Sie, dass kein Kaffee herauskommt.

Der Ausgießer könnte blockiert sein. Fragen Sie, ob Ihr Partner den Kaffee herausgekratzt hat.

Bejahen Sie und sagen Sie, dass die Maschine trotzdem nicht funktioniert.

Fragen Sie, ob die Maschine eingesteckt ist.

Bejahen Sie.

Sagen Sie, dass der Ausgießer kaputt ist. Ihr Partner soll per E-Mail einen neuen Ausgießer anfordern.

Bedanken und verabschieden Sie sich.

Verabschieden Sie sich.

D   Schreiben Sie eine kurze E-Mail an Fando Electrical. Erklären Sie Ihr Problem und bitten Sie um Zusendung eines neuen Ausgießers.

USEFUL LANGUAGE

I'm calling because we're having problems with …
It's model number …
We've already …, but … still doesn't work.
Thank you very much for your help.

THE SITUATION You and a colleague have to order a new table for your office. A water cooler and a tray for glasses will sit on top of it.

The water cooler is 37 centimetres deep, 39 centimetres wide and 115 centimetres high. With water, it weighs 32 kilogrammes. The capacity of the water cooler bottle is 19 litres.
The tray is 35 centimetres long and 26 centimetres wide.

1 Ordering products with measurements

A Beschreiben Sie mithilfe der rechts stehenden ‚Useful language'-Box die Gegenstände auf den Bildern oben. Worum handelt es sich? Wie sind die genauen Maße und wie ist das Gewicht?

USEFUL LANGUAGE

It is a …
It is … cm long/wide/high/deep.
It weighs … kg.
Its capacity is … litres.

B Entscheiden Sie zusammen mit einem Partner, welche Maße Ihr Tisch haben muss und wie viel Gewicht er tragen muss. Schreiben Sie dazu einen Satz auf Englisch und lesen Sie ihn Ihrem Partner vor.

I think the table must be … cm wide, … cm long and … cm high. It needs to hold … kg.

C Schreiben Sie eine E-Mail an Herrn Furnish in der Einkaufsabteilung **(Purchasing department)** Ihrer Firma. Bitten Sie ihn, einen Tisch mit Ihren in 1B ermittelten Maßen zu bestellen. Nennen Sie die Maße und bitten Sie ihn, den Preis für einen solchen Tisch – inklusive Lieferung – herauszufinden. Empfehlen Sie ergonomika.com als Onlineshop mit einer guten Auswahl an günstigen Tischen. Achten Sie auf die korrekte Form (Betreff, Anrede, Schlussformel).

KMK

NEW SITUATION

Ergonomika has delivered the table to your offices. Now you and a colleague have to check that all the parts are there and none are missing.

2 | Dealing with products with many parts

A Arbeiten Sie mit einem Partner. Partner A blättert zu File 11 auf S. 138, Partner B zu File 14 auf S. 139.

B Sie müssen wegen der fehlenden Teile Ergonomika anrufen. Schauen Sie sich die folgenden Ausdrücke aus einer automatischen Telefonansage an. Entscheiden Sie in Partnerarbeit, was diese Aussagen bedeuten könnten.

1 Please choose one of the following options.
2 If you are calling about an existing order, press two.
3 Please enter your customer ID.
4 For all other enquiries, press star.

1/31

C Hören Sie sich die Telefonoptionen der Kundenservice-Hotline von Ergonomika an und schreiben Sie das Folgende auf:

Schritt 1 bis 4: Notieren Sie, welche Nummer Sie wählen sollen.
Schritt 5 bis 7: Notieren Sie, welche Informationen Sie eingeben sollen.
Schritt 8: Notieren Sie, wann die Firma Ihnen das neue Teil zusenden wird.

CULTURE

Calling a hotline

Most hotlines begin with a menu, asking you either to press a number or to say it. One of the menu options will be to connect to a customer service representative. When you connect with a customer service representative, that person will probably be Indian! Most companies in the UK and USA outsource their call centres to India, because employees there are cheaper, and they also speak English. Indians have different accents than the British or the Americans. If you don't talk to Indians very often, you might need to ask the customer service representative to repeat what he or she says.

> **THE SITUATION** Claudia is a German cook who has started her own catering business in New York. She wants to cater for events and parties but she needs a marketing plan.

1 | Choosing a form of advertising

A Welche Arten von Werbung kennen Sie? Übertragen Sie die Mindmap auf ein Blatt Papier und fügen Sie gemeinsam mit einem Partner Ihre eigenen Ideen hinzu.

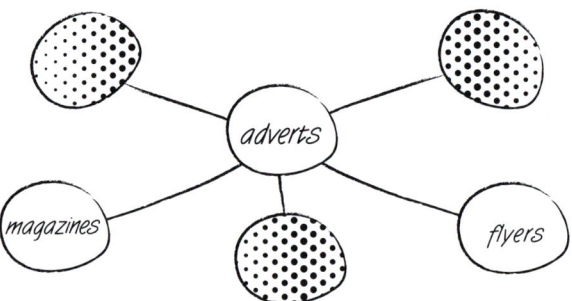

1/32

B Hören Sie den ersten Teil eines Gesprächs zwischen Claudia und dem Marketingberater John. Wählen Sie die richtige Antwort aus.

1 Claudia does not cater for
  a children's parties and birthdays.
  b communions.

2 The advisor thinks Claudia's list of services is
  a too short.
  b too long.

3 Claudia
  a hates baking.
  b loves baking.

4 Claudia prefers weddings because
  a she likes to wear nice clothes.
  b everybody is really happy.

5 The food is very important at
  a weddings.
  b company events.

1/33

C Hören Sie den zweiten Teil des Gesprächs und machen Sie sich Notizen zu den verschiedenen Arten von Werbung, die John nennt.

D Hören Sie sich das Gespräch noch einmal an und beantworten Sie die Fragen.

1 What advertising does Claudia do?
2 How do Claudia's customers contact her?
3 Where does John say Claudia should advertise?
4 What is the problem with wedding magazines?
5 Which keyword is not good?

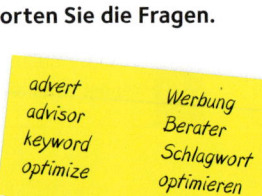

advert	Werbung
advisor	Berater
keyword	Schlagwort
optimize	optimieren

2 | Creating an internet advert

A Schauen Sie sich die Internetanzeigen an und benennen Sie die verschiedenen Elemente.

Parts of an internet advert:
- headline (35 letters maximum)
- text (70 letters maximum)
- website address

A
[Wedding make-up](www.superweddingmakeup.com)
Top-quality make-up for that special day!
www.superweddingmakeup.com

B
[Bikes for sale!](www.bikesnmore.co.uk)
Thousands of bikes at low prices.
Biggest choice in the UK.
www.bikesnmore.co.uk

C
[Corporate catering](www.cateringcorporate.co.uk)
Business meetings, product launches, special events.
www.cateringcorporate.co.uk

B Wählen Sie drei Schlagwörter, die für Claudias Internetanzeige gut geeignet wären und begründen Sie Ihre Entscheidung. Erstellen Sie auf dieser Grundlage eine Internetanzeige für Claudias Firma. Verwenden Sie die Beispiele in 2A als Vorlage.

> bride • bridegroom • cake • catering • cheap • corporate • dinner • flowers • fun •
> Germany • high-quality • lunch • marriage • New York • wedding

C Entwerfen Sie eine Anzeige für eine Dienstleistung, die von einer Ihnen bekannten Firma angeboten wird. Verwenden Sie die Beispiele in 2A als Vorlage.

D Schauen Sie sich den unten stehenden Flyer eines Caterers in New York an. Entwerfen Sie einen ähnlichen Flyer für eine Firma, die Sie kennen.

Wedding Catering
From the meal to the cake –
You don't have to worry
about a thing!

Call
The New York Caterers
on
555-8675 4732

www.newyorkcaterers.com

(THE SITUATION) Your boss gives you some product brochures. He asks you to design a similar brochure for one of your company's products.

1 | Understanding brochures

A Welche Informationen finden Sie üblicherweise in Produktbroschüren? Lesen Sie die Broschüren und erstellen Sie eine Liste der darin gemachten Angaben.

type of product, model number, ...

UNIVERSAL TABLET PC

The Universal Tablet PC has a fantastic design. It uses the Android operating system. You can play games, write e-mails, use the internet or watch movies. And it's very easy to use!

MODEL NUMBER:	UP4546-A	CERTIFICATION:	ENERGY STAR
WEIGHT:	380 GRAMS	CAMERA:	8.0 MEGAPIXEL
OPERATING SYSTEM:	ANDROID	WIRELESS:	802.11 B/G/N
BATTERY LIFE:	18 HOURS	PRICE:	€ 499
MEMORY:	64 GB		

FANDO
Easy Slide Steam Iron

Fando irons give only the best results. The Fando Easy Slide Steam Iron uses advanced technology and makes ironing fun.

Model number:	FE4935678
Steam output:	40 grams/minute
Steam booster:	120 grams/minute
Power output:	1500 watts
Certification:	Blue Angel
Features:	Soft rubber handle
Price:	**€ 85.99**

Black Star Cordless Sander

The Black Star Cordless Sander sands all types of wood and metal. It's Energy Star rated for a better environment and it's very light and comfortable to use.

Model number:	BSC-878635
Battery voltage:	7.2 V
Sanding surface:	127 cm²
Features:	Micro-filter system
Weight:	0.7 kg
Certification:	Energy Star
Price:	**€ 69.95**

feature	*Merkmal*
memory	*Speicher*
operating system	*Betriebssystem*
power output	*Leistung*
surface	*Oberfläche*

B Schauen Sie sich die Broschüren noch einmal an. Sprechen Sie mit einem Partner über die technischen Daten und die Vorteile der Produkte. Verwenden Sie die ,Useful language'-Box auf S. 53 als Hilfe.

2 | Describing products and functions

Partnerarbeit: Wählen Sie eines der beiden Produkte und lesen Sie die Produkt-
beschreibung. Stellen Sie sich gegenseitig die folgenden Fragen und beschreiben Sie
einander Ihre Produkte. Verwenden Sie die ‚Useful language'-Box als Hilfe.

Partner A

Model number:	CD3425
Features:	FM digital radio, CD player
Dimensions:	20 cm x 30 cm x 23 cm
Power:	500 watts
Price:	€ 249

Partner B

Model number:	XPS32
Features:	Scanner, printer, fax
Dimensions:	40 cm x 61 cm x 92 cm
Power:	80 watts
Price:	€ 325

1 What product is it?
2 What can you do with it?
3 What is its length/width/height?

4 How much power does it have?
5 How much does it cost?
6 Would you buy it? Why, or why not?

3 | Designing and presenting brochures

A **Wählen Sie ein Produkt aus, das von Ihrer Firma hergestellt wird oder das Sie bei
der Arbeit benutzen. Machen Sie sich Notizen zum Aussehen, zu den technischen
Daten und zu anderen Merkmalen, von denen Sie meinen, sie könnten für eine
englischsprachige Broschüre wichtig sein.**

B **Entwerfen Sie für Ihr Produkt eine Broschüre. Nennen Sie die relevanten Produkt-
informationen und bewerben Sie die Vorteile des Produkts. Verwenden Sie als
Hilfe die Beispiele aus 1A und 2 sowie die ‚Useful language'-Box.**

C **Wählen Sie ein Produkt, das jeder in der Klasse kennt (z. B. ein Handy oder eine
Bohrmaschine) und notieren Sie sich Stichpunkte, mit denen Sie das Produkt
beschreiben können. Stellen Sie das Produkt der Klasse vor, ohne das Produkt zu
benennen. Lassen Sie Ihre Mitschüler raten, um welches Produkt es sich handelt.**

USEFUL LANGUAGE

It's … cm long by … cm wide by … cm high.

It weighs … grammes/kilogrammes.

It has a battery life of … hours / a 16 GB memory / a 8.0 megapixel camera.

The power output is …

It looks modern/stylish/fantastic.

It's easy/comfortable to use.

THE SITUATION You have to present your company to a group of new trainees.

1 Marketing

A Schauen Sie sich die Firmenlogos an. Stellen Sie fest, um welche Art von Firma es sich jeweils handelt, und welche Produkte oder Dienstleistungen sie anbietet. Machen Sie Aussagen wie diese:

1 *McDonald's is an American fast food chain. It sells burgers and has restaurants all over the world. Its most popular product is the Big Mac.*

1 **2** **3** **4**

B Wo kann man die Logos aus 1A sehen? Fügen Sie Ihre eigenen Ideen zu den folgenden Vorschlägen hinzu.

Magazines	Merchandise	Online	Posters	Television
▪ on the cover	▪ T-shirts	▪ in social networks	▪ in the street	▪ on the news

2 Presenting a company

A Überfliegen Sie die Präsentationsfolien auf S. 55 und ordnen Sie die folgenden Beschreibungen (a–d) den Folien (1–4) zu.

a Detailed information
b History and overview
c What the company produces
d How the company advertises

B Lesen Sie jetzt die Folien auf S. 55 genau durch und beantworten Sie die Fragen.

1 How old is the company Daimler?
2 Where are the company's headquarters?
3 How many employees does Daimler have?
4 When was the company's most popular car made?
5 Where does the company advertise?

> billboard — Reklametafel
> manufacturer — Hersteller
> merchandise — Handelsware

1/34

C Hören Sie eine Firmenvorstellung von Daimler. In welcher Reihenfolge werden die Folien in dieser Präsentation verwendet? Machen Sie sich Notizen.

D Hören Sie die Präsentation noch einmal und notieren Sie sich nützliche Ausdrücke für eine Firmenpräsentation.

E Gruppenarbeit: Wählen Sie eine der Firmen aus 1A und entwerfen Sie für sie eine Präsentation ähnlich wie die über Daimler. Recherchieren Sie dazu weitere Informationen über die gewählte Firma im Internet.

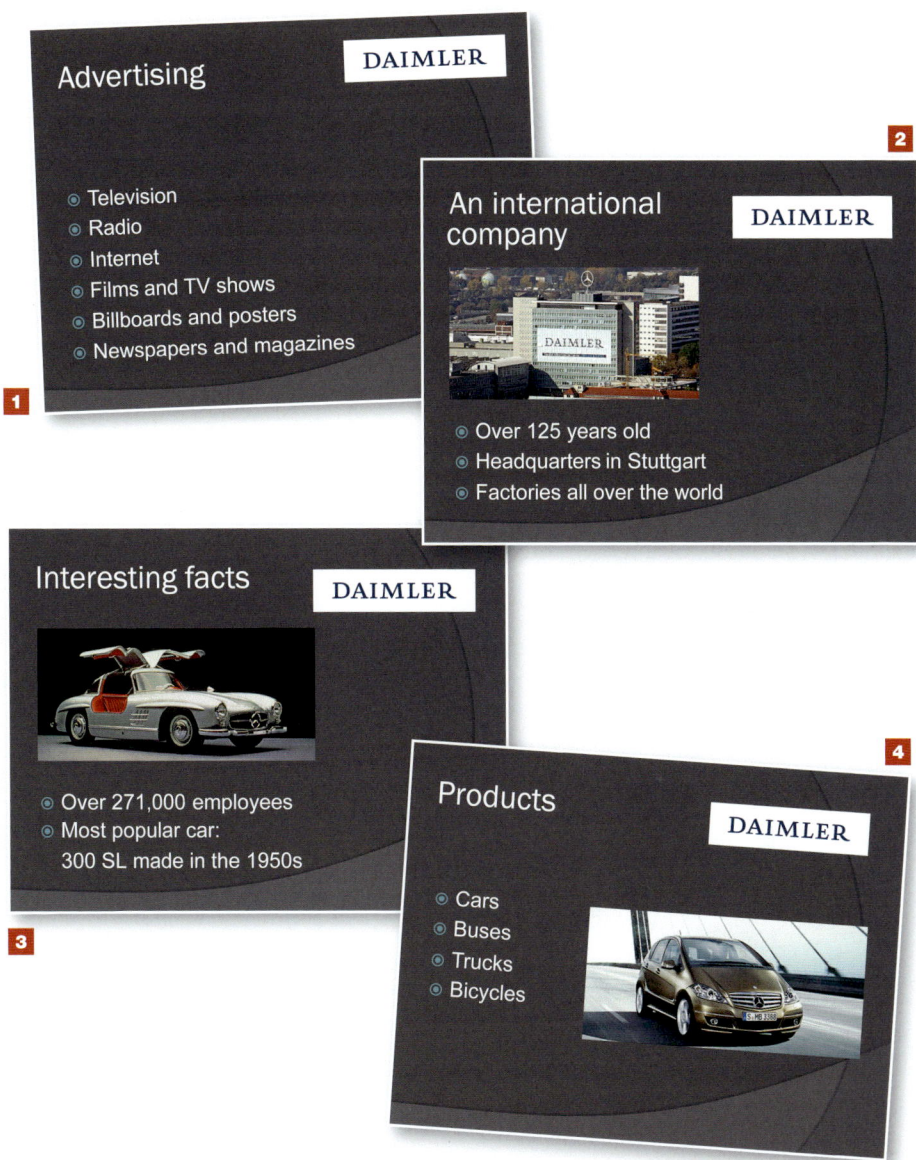

3 | Presenting your own company

Notieren Sie sich einige wichtige Fakten über Ihre eigene Firma oder eine Firma, die Sie kennen. Berücksichtigen Sie dabei die folgenden Aspekte. Stellen Sie anschließend die Firma auf Englisch in der Klasse vor.

- Was die Firma tut oder herstellt
- Wo die Firma Ihre Hauptniederlassung hat
- Ob es eine lokale, nationale oder internationale Firma ist
- Die Anzahl der Angestellten
- Das wichtigste Produkt der Firma
- Wo und wie die Firma Werbung macht

Lerntipp

Vokabeln im Zusammenhang lernen

Anstatt Vokabeln einzeln zu lernen, ist es oft wirksamer, sie im Zusammenhang (als Teil einer Redewendung oder eines ganzen Satzes) zu lernen. So merken Sie sich nicht nur die Bedeutung der Vokabel, sondern auch, wie sie gebraucht wird.

Test 1

Vervollständigen Sie die Sätze mit den Wörtern in der Box.

> comfortable (p. 40) • van (p. 40) • difficult (p. 41) • expensive (p. 43) • work (p. 46)

1 For my job as a taxi driver, I need a car that has room and is …
2 1,000 euros! That's a very … printer!
3 This … seats eight people.
4 I pressed the button but the machine didn't …
5 Speaking a foreign language can sometimes be really …

Test 2

Suchen Sie die zusammengehörigen Wörter, um geläufige Ausdrücke und Wendungen zu bilden.

A

1	long-	a	guide (p. 40)
2	tour	b	quality brand (p. 43)
3	high-	c	lasting (p. 44)
4	missing	d	part (p. 49)
5	like to wear	e	nice clothes (p. 50)

B

1	advertise in newspapers	a	events (p. 51)
2	fast food	b	system (p. 52)
3	cater for special	c	technology (p. 52)
4	Android operating	d	chain (p. 54)
5	use advanced	e	and magazines (p. 55)

Test 3

Überlegen Sie sich zu den folgenden Vokabeln jeweils einen Beispielsatz, durch den die Bedeutung des Wortes klar wird.

1 weigh (p. 48) *My rucksack weighs a ton!*
2 deliver (p. 49)
3 customer (p. 50)
4 advert (p. 50)
5 company (p. 54)

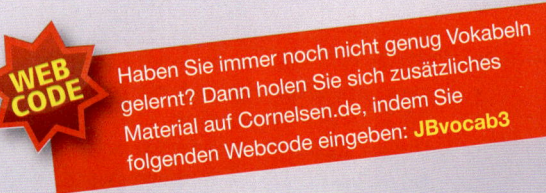

WEB CODE Haben Sie immer noch nicht genug Vokabeln gelernt? Dann holen Sie sich zusätzliches Material auf Cornelsen.de, indem Sie folgenden Webcode eingeben: **JBvocab3**

Produktion: Schriftstücke erstellen

ALLGEMEINE INFORMATIONEN ZUM PRÜFUNGSTEIL

Dieser Teil der Prüfung macht 30 % der Punktewerte der schriftlichen Prüfung aus. Hier müssen Sie zeigen, dass Sie in der Lage sind, eine berufliche E-Mail, einen Geschäftsbrief oder ein Fax zu schreiben. Dabei ist es wichtig, dass Sie alle Inhalte, die in der Aufgabenstellung vorgegeben werden, in Ihrem Text berücksichtigen. Achten Sie insbesondere auf eine korrekte Anrede, Form und Schlussformel. Sie dürfen für die Bearbeitung der Aufgabe ein zweisprachiges Wörterbuch benutzen. Nehmen Sie sich für diese Aufgabe etwa 15 Minuten Zeit. Auf dieser Seite finden Sie zwei Aufgaben dieses Typs.

1

Ihr Vorgesetzter Herr Schmitt benötigt die aktuellen Kataloge und Preislisten der Firma Jingfan Import/Export Co. Ltd. Er bittet Sie deshalb, eine E-Mail auf Englisch an die chinesische Firma zu schreiben, in der Sie diese Unterlagen anfordern. Berücksichtigen Sie dabei die folgenden Punkte:

- wählen Sie eine geeignete Betreffzeile für Ihre Anfrage;
- finden Sie eine korrekte Anrede für die Empfängerin der E-Mail, Frau Jingjing Wang;
- nehmen Sie Bezug auf das Treffen zwischen Frau Jingjing Wang und Herrn Schmitt auf der Frankfurter Messe letzte Woche;
- bitten Sie um Zusendung der aktuellen Kataloge und Preislisten;
- fragen Sie, ob Jingfan Import/Export Co. Ltd. bereits Verkaufsvertreter in Deutschland hat;
- sagen Sie, dass Sie sich freuen, bald von der Firma zu hören und verabschieden Sie sich in angemessener Form.

2

Ihre Firma wartet dringend auf eine Lieferung der irischen Firma ABC Ireland (Adresse: 22 Sandyford Road, Dublin 12). Ihre Vorgesetzte bittet Sie, ein Fax auf Englisch an John McGurk (Faxnummer: +353 1 587 3290) mit folgendem Inhalt zu schreiben:

- nehmen Sie Bezug auf Ihre Bestellung vom 15.5. diesen Jahres, Auftragsnummer 827/RT;
- der vereinbarte Liefertermin war der 26.6., heute ist schon der 7.7., und Sie haben immer noch keine Lieferung erhalten;
- Sie haben schon mehrmals versucht, den Lieferanten telefonisch zu erreichen, aber bis jetzt ohne Erfolg;
- bitten Sie um sofortige Zusendung der überfälligen Lieferung;
- verlangen Sie eine umgehende Bestätigung des Warenversandes.

Schreiben Sie das Fax und achten Sie auf die korrekte Form (Adresskopf, Anrede, Betreff, Schlussformel).

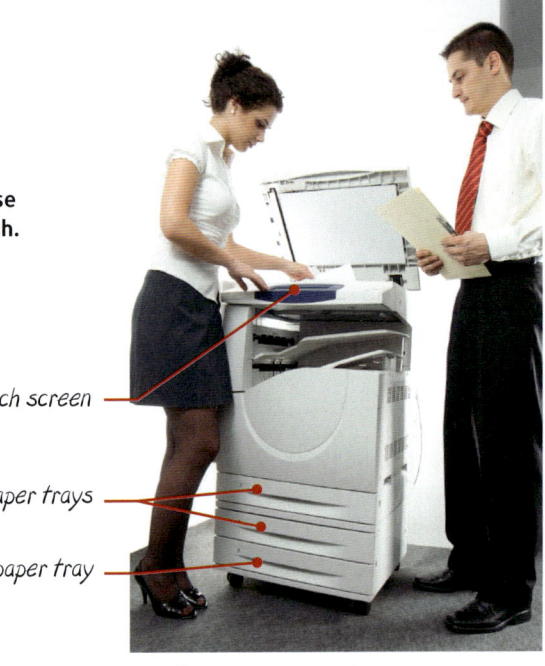

THE SITUATION

Eva Bach works for the company Besterman in Germany. A trainee, Peter de Witt, has come from Besterman's branch in the Netherlands, and he doesn't speak German! Eva teaches him how to use the office's photocopier – in English.

touch screen

A4 paper trays

A3 paper tray

1 Understanding an instruction manual

A Ordnen Sie die Anweisungen a-g im Benutzerhandbuch den Symbolen 1-7 auf dem Touch-Screen zu. Sie müssen noch nicht jedes Wort verstehen.

a Enter the number of copies that you need.
b Turn on the photocopier and give it time to warm up.
c Check the paper level in the paper tray.
d Close the cover and press the 'Start' button.
e Select black-and-white or colour copying.
f Choose the correct paper size, for example, A3 or A4.
g Open the cover and place the document carefully in the correct position on the glass.

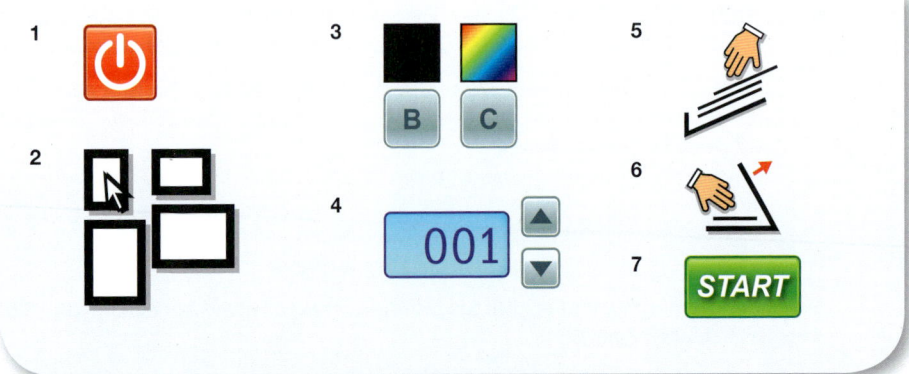

B Prüfen Sie jetzt, ob Sie die <mark>gelb markierten</mark> Wörter in den Anweisungen richtig verstehen: Ordnen Sie ihnen die folgenden Übersetzungen zu.

Taste • Füllstand • eingeben • Abdeckhaube • legen • Fach • Größe • wählen • aufwärmen

1/35

C Lesen Sie Peters Fragen und ordnen Sie ihnen die richtigen Antworten (a–g) aus dem Benutzerhandbuch zu. Hören Sie sich dann den Dialog an, um Ihre Antworten zu überprüfen.

Peter	So how do I get started?
Eva (1)	⏻ *First, turn on the photocopier and give it time to warm up.*
Peter	So where do I put the document for copying?
Eva (2)	🖐↗
Peter	What about the size of paper?
Eva (3)	▣▢
Peter	And what do I do about colour or black-and-white?
Eva (4)	■▨ B C
Peter	But how do I know if there's enough paper?
Eva (5)	🖐
Peter	OK, and how do I get the right number of copies?
Eva (6)	001 ▲▼
Peter	And what do I do after that?
Eva (7)	START

REMEMBER

How do I …
Where you …
What

2 | Giving and understanding instructions

★ **A** Spielen Sie den Dialog von Peter und Eva mit einem Partner nach. Lesen Sie den Text möglichst nicht ab, sondern benutzen Sie nur die Abbildungen 1–7 aus Aufgabe 1A als Anhaltspunkte.

YOUR CHOICE

★★ **B** Erklären Sie Ihrem Partner auf Englisch die Benutzung eines Geräts, das Sie auf der Arbeit verwenden, z. B. einer Kaffeemaschine oder Ihres Handys.

✈ **C** Die Kollegen geben verschiedene Kopien in Auftrag. Eva benutzt dies als praktische Übung für Peter. Spielen Sie mit einem Partner die entsprechenden Dialoge. Verwenden Sie die Ausdrücke, die Sie bereits gelernt haben. Fangen Sie so an:

Eva	So, what do you do first?
Peter	First, I turn on the photocopier and give it time to warm up.
Eva	Right. And what do you do next?

Eva, I need 10 copies of this document, in colour and in A3. And it's urgent!

Can I please have 15 A4 copies, black-and-white ASAP?*

*ASAP = as soon as possible

> **THE SITUATION** You work in a kitchen with colleagues from other countries. Everyone speaks English and uses recipes in English. People need to explain the recipes to each other. You want to make these two recipes, but in larger versions: 60 brownies and 40 servings of spaghetti Bolognese.

Nut and Chocolate Chip Brownies
Makes 15.

150 g chocolate
120 ml sunflower oil
215 g brown sugar
2 eggs
1 teaspoon vanilla extract

1 package (15 g) baking powder
4 tablespoons cocoa powder
75 g chopped walnuts
60 g milk chocolate chips

1 Lightly grease a 19 cm square cake tin.
2 Chop the plain chocolate.
3 Melt chocolate in a bowl over a pan of hot water.
4 First, mix together the oil, sugar, eggs and vanilla extract. Add the melted chocolate and beat well. Then, add the baking powder and cocoa powder and stir until well mixed. Finally, add the chopped nuts and milk chocolate chips and mix again.
5 Pour the mixture evenly into the cake tin.
6 Bake for about 30–35 minutes at 180°.
7 Cool in the tin.
8 Cut into squares.

Spaghetti Bolognese
Makes 4 servings.

800 g spaghetti
2 onions
1 tbsp olive oil

350 g mincemeat (beef or pork)
500 ml Bolognese sauce
30 g Parmesan cheese

1 Peel onions and chop finely.
2 Fry onions in a frying pan with olive oil.
3 Add mincemeat and fry until brown. Stir often.
4 Add Bolognese sauce and mix well.
5 Heat water in a pot until it boils.
6 Add spaghetti to boiling water. Cook for 10 minutes. Stir occasionally.
7 Strain the spaghetti.
8 Grate Parmesan cheese.
9 Serve the noodles on a plate. Then add the sauce and, finally, the grated cheese.

beat	schlagen
grease	einfetten
mix	mischen
peel	schälen
stir	rühren

1 | Ordering supplies

Arbeiten Sie in einer Gruppe von mindestens drei Personen. Berechnen Sie zunächst anhand der beiden Rezepte, wie viel von jeder Zutat gebraucht wird. Stellen Sie dann fest, was Sie beim Lieferanten bestellen müssen. Einiges haben Sie schon vorrätig (siehe Bild unten).

	product	size	quantity
a	baking powder	500 g	?
b	Bolognese sauce	5 l	?
c	brown sugar	5 kg	?
d	chocolate	500 g	?
e	chocolate chips	1 kg	?
f	cocoa powder	500 g	?
g	eggs	20	?
h	mincemeat (beef)	1 kg	?
i	olive oil	5 l	?
j	onions	5 kg	?
k	Parmesan cheese	500 g	?
l	spaghetti	5 kg	?
m	sunflower oil	5 l	?
n	vanilla extract	250 ml	?
o	walnuts, chopped	1 kg	?

USEFUL LANGUAGE

We need one kilogramme of …   We've already got some …
We (don't) have enough …   We haven't got any …

REMEMBER

We've got **some** …
We have**n't** got **any** …

2 | Understanding and explaining recipes

A   Arbeiten Sie mit einem Partner. Erklären Sie sich gegenseitig jeden Arbeitsschritt von einem der beiden Rezepte auf Deutsch.

B   Schreiben Sie ein eigenes Rezept für eines der folgenden Gerichte.

YOUR CHOICE

★
vegetable soup
fruit salad
scrambled eggs
fried potatoes

★★
salad with chicken breast and a dressing
asparagus and pancakes
stir-fry vegetables and rice
hamburger on a bun with lettuce, tomato, etc.

THE SITUATION PowerWay is preparing the packaging design for its new PW24-1A cordless power drill. The designer has finished the layout. Now it's time to add the texts which describe the features.

A Arbeiten Sie mit einem Partner und ordnen Sie die Produktmerkmale (a–f) den Abbildungen (1–6) zu. Nennen Sie die Stichworte, die Ihnen bei der Zuordnung geholfen haben.

a Fast and slow speeds give you the flexibility you need for many sorts of job.
b Two batteries help you complete longer jobs without stopping.
c The 24-volt motor offers all the power you need for the biggest jobs.
d With the free 36-piece set of drill bits you can drill wood, metal, glass and even ceramic tiles.
e Wall plugs included!
f The screwdriver bit lets you drive a screw in just seconds.

PW24-1A cordless power drill

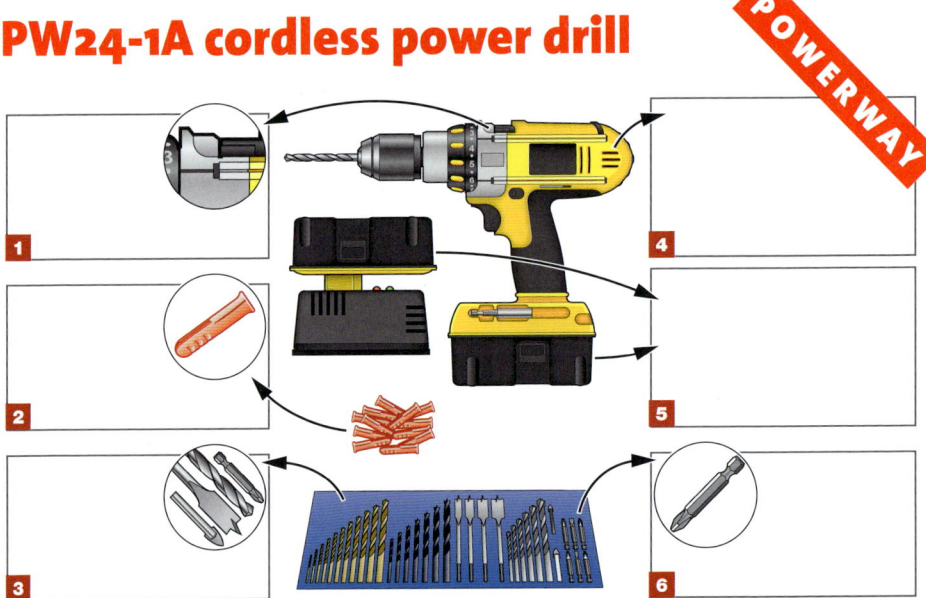

POWERWAY

B Finden Sie mit Ihrem Partner die deutsche Bedeutung der hervorgehobenen Wörter. Verwenden Sie dazu die Bilder als Hilfe.

Akkus • bohren • Bohrerspitzen • Dübel • Geschwindigkeiten • Holz • Keramikfliesen • Schraube • Schraubenzieher

C Übersetzen Sie mit Ihrem Partner die Produktmerkmale in 1A. Der Text soll auf die Verpackung der Kartons für den deutschen Markt gedruckt werden.

NEW SITUATION Your company has moved into new offices and you have to hang some pictures. Sven, a colleague from Sweden, is giving you tips on how to use the power drill.

D   Lesen Sie Svens Tipps (1–6) und ordnen Sie ihnen die Bilder (a–f) zu.

1 Put some ==tape== around the drill bit to show how deep you need to drill.

2 ==Mark== the place where you need to drill.

3 For a soft material, e.g. a normal wall, use a hammer and a nail punch to make a small hole on the mark. Now the drill bit won't ==slip== away from the mark.

4 For a harder material, e.g. a ceramic tile, ==cover== the mark with 'see-through' tape. This helps to stop the drill bit from slipping away from the mark.

5 Start drilling at low speed to start the hole correctly, and then go faster.

6 Be careful to keep the drill at 90 ==degrees== to the wall.

> e.g.   z.B.
> nail punch   Nageltreiber

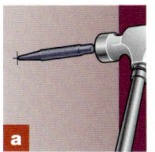 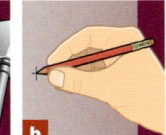  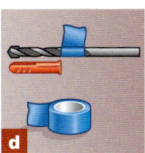  

a   b   c   d   e   f

E   Finden Sie mit Ihrem Partner die deutsche Bedeutung der ==hervorgehobenen== Wörter. Verwenden Sie dazu die Bilder als Hilfe.

> abdecken • abrutschen • Grad • Klebeband • markieren

F   Verfassen Sie mit Ihrem Partner auf der Grundlage von Svens Hinweisen einige Tipps für das deutsche Benutzerhandbuch für den neuen PowerWay-Bohrer. Fangen Sie wie folgt an:

Top-Tipps – Wie Sie das Beste aus Ihrem neuen PowerWay24-1A herausholen können.
Beachten Sie die folgenden Punkte und es kann (fast) nichts mehr schiefgehen.
a   ...

G   Schauen Sie sich die Bilderfolge an und schreiben Sie die zugehörige Anleitung.

How to drill ceramic tiles

  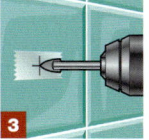  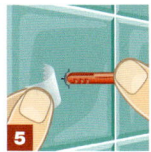 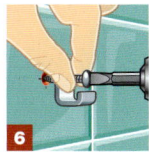

1   2   3   4   5   6

ceramic drill bit   normal drill bit

THE SITUATION Anders Jorgensen is the training manager at Western Engineering. He is worried because some trainees are leaving their workspace dirty and untidy at night, and he must do something to stop this.

1 Understanding an announcement

A Herr Jorgensen hat Bilder von den Arbeitsbereichen seiner Auszubildenden gemacht. Damit möchte er zeigen, wie man einen Arbeitsplatz richtig und wie man ihn falsch hinterlässt. Schauen Sie sich die beiden Bilder an, die er an das schwarze Brett geheftet hat und beschreiben Sie die Unterschiede.

B Herr Jorgensen hat neben die Bilder einen Aushang geheftet. Lesen Sie ihn durch und sagen Sie der Person, die den Arbeitsplatz auf Bild 1 benutzt, was sie tun sollte und was sie nicht tun darf.

REMEMBER

You **shouldn't leave** the lights on.
You **must switch off** the power.

IMPORTANT NOTICE TO ALL TRAINEES

FROM: THE MANAGER
SUBJECT: MAKING OUR WORKSPACE A BETTER PLACE

I have noticed that some trainees are leaving their workspaces in a terrible mess at night. For example, just look at picture 1. This must stop!

Please remember the rules:
- First, we have our rules for a clean and tidy workplace. This means you must clean up, tidy up and put away all hand tools before you leave work. You should not leave any tools on your workbench at night. You should also empty your rubbish bin, and you must not leave cables or rubbish on the floor.
- Next, there are our rules about energy and resources. You should not leave the lights on at night. It also means you must turn off all equipment and switch off the power.
- Finally, I have two other points. Our training staff need to know what work you have done. That means you must not forget to complete your timesheet at the end of every day. You should also return dirty overalls for cleaning.

I'm sure you all understand that these things are important. Please make them happen – as in picture 2!

Anders Jorgensen

1

2

resources	Ressourcen
rubbish bin	Mülleimer
timesheet	Stundennachweis
tool	Werkzeug
workbench	Werkbank

NEW SITUATION There is a kitchen at the training centre, and there need to be rules here too.

2 | Explaining and writing rules

A Schauen Sie sich mit einem Partner auf dem Bild oben die Dinge an, die richtig oder falsch gemacht werden. Benutzen Sie die folgenden Vorgaben und erklären Sie sich gegenseitig die Küchenregeln.

> **REMEMBER**
>
> **Clean** the table after you use it.
> **Don't overfill** the fridge.

	clean	all dirty dishes and put them in the cupboard.
	overfill	empty cans and bottles in the recycling bin.
Please (don't)	put	energy: turn off the lights when you leave.
	wash	the fridge or the freezer.
	waste	the table after you use it.

B Schreiben Sie einen Aushang für deutsche Besucher, auf dem Sie die Regeln aus 2A als Dos und Don'ts auflisten.   `KMK`

DOS	DONTS
Bitte säubern Sie …	*Bitte … Sie nicht …*

★ **C** Erstellen Sie in Gruppenarbeit eine Liste mit sechs Regeln für Ihren Arbeitsplatz oder für Ihre Schule. Verwenden Sie jedes der folgenden Wörter mindestens zwei Mal: *must, should* und *please*.

★★ **D** Schreiben Sie auf Englisch einen Aushang für das schwarze Brett mit mindestens fünf Regeln für Ihren Arbeitsplatz oder Ihre Schule. Nehmen Sie Herrn Jorgensens Aushang aus 1B als Vorlage.

✈ **E** Überlegen Sie sich eine zusätzliche Regel, die es an Ihrem Arbeitsplatz oder an Ihrer Schule noch nicht gibt, von der Sie aber denken, dass sie nützlich wäre. Schreiben Sie sie auf. Fragen Sie andere, ob sie Ihrer Regel zustimmen.

Germany

Dubai

United Arab Emirates

THE SITUATION

Dubai, part of the United Arab Emirates, is growing fast because of its many industries. Companies there are bringing in workers from all over the world. You work for an employment agency that finds people from Germany for jobs in Dubai.

1 Understanding dress requirements

A Schauen Sie sich die Fotos oben an. Welcher Art von Arbeit gehen die Menschen nach? Was passiert in jeder dieser Arbeitssituationen? Was glauben Sie, warum die Beschäftigten so angezogen sind?

B Lesen Sie die drei Überschriften zu Informationen für neue Mitarbeiter. Was glauben Sie, welche der abgebildeten Kleidungsstücke (1–9) die drei unterschiedlichen Berufsgruppen tragen müssen? Formulieren Sie Aussagen wie diese:

1   Sales staff have to wear grey jackets and ties.

1 Dress code for sales staff in Dubai
2 Clothing for construction site workers
3 Laboratory staff: dress requirements

construction site	Baustelle
employment agency	Arbeitsvermittlung
jewellery	Schmuck
label	beschriften
provide	zur Verfügung stellen
requirement	Anforderung

1 cap

2 face mask

3 hard hat

4 'high-vis' jacket

5 jacket

6 lab coat

7 latex gloves

8 safety boots

9 tie

C   Überfliegen Sie die Textauszüge und ordnen Sie sie den Überschriften in 1B zu.

A

A construction site can be a dangerous place, so all workers must follow these rules:

- Always wear a hard hat.
- Wear safety boots at all times.
- Always wear yellow overalls and a 'high-vis' jacket.

The company will provide hard hats, overalls and 'high-vis' jackets, but workers must provide their own safety boots. New staff who arrive for work without the right boots will not be allowed to go on site.

B

As we operate in a sterile work environment, we do everything possible to keep it as clean as we can. This means that staff must wear face masks and caps to cover their hair. We also ask workers to change into sterile shoes when they enter the lab, and they must wear sterile latex gloves to work on our products. We provide these items of clothing for all employees, but we ask them to provide three white lab coats. The company offers a free cleaning service for everyone, so staff must label their coats clearly with their name and lab number.

C

We want to show our customers that we are a friendly and efficient team, always ready to help. This means that all staff must dress neatly at all times. We provide jackets in the company colour of grey, as well as ties. Male staff should wear black trousers and female staff should wear black skirts that are knee-length. Shirts and blouses should be white, shoes must be black. Male staff must wear their hair short. Any jewellery must be minimal and discreet.

D   Notieren Sie auf Deutsch die wichtigsten Punkte aus den Texten (A–C) für   `KMK`
     Personen, die in diesen drei Jobs arbeiten werden. Verwenden Sie dazu die
     folgende Tabelle.

1. Kleidungsstücke, die die Firma zur Verfügung stellt	2. Ausstattung, die der Angestellte selbst beisteuern muss	3. Spezielle Anforderungen und Warnhinweise

2 | Comparing dress codes

A   Partnerarbeit: Vergleichen Sie die Kleidungsvorschriften an Ihren jeweiligen
     Arbeitsplätzen. Berücksichtigen Sie dabei die folgenden Fragen.

   1   What do people have to wear (if anything in particular)?
   2   What are people allowed and not allowed to wear?
   3   Why do you think your workplace has these rules?

✈ B   Vergleichen Sie in Partnerarbeit die Kleidungsvorschriften an Ihrem eigenen
       Arbeitsplatz mit denen bei einer der drei Firmen in Dubai. Beschreiben Sie
       Gemeinsamkeiten und Unterschiede.

  C   Berichten Sie der Klasse, was Sie über die Kleidungsvorschriften am Arbeitsplatz
       Ihres Partners erfahren haben.

THE SITUATION You have a summer job in a busy kitchen in a foreign country. A few minutes ago a colleague dropped a glass bottle of olive oil on the floor. 'Oh, dear! That's a pity!' he said, and went to the storage room to get another bottle. Another colleague was cutting vegetables at a nearby counter. Unfortunately, she has slipped on the oil and has cut her arm with her knife. It's bleeding now, quite badly. You remember from your emergency training what to do.

General information in case of an emergency

» Stay calm.
» Take the injured person away from the dangerous area.
» Block off the dangerous area.
» Mind your own safety.
» Call the emergency hotline.

Calling the emergency hotline

Be prepared to answer the following questions.
» WHERE did the accident happen?
» WHAT happened?
» HOW MANY are injured?

» WHAT kind(s) of injuries and symptoms are there? For example:

not breathing

not conscious

bleeding

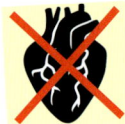
heart not beating

WAIT for further questions and requests!

1 | Mediation in an emergency

A In der Küche arbeitet noch ein weiterer deutscher Muttersprachler. Sagen Sie ihm, was er in diesem Notfall tun muss. Beziehen Sie sich dabei auf die Situationsbeschreibung und auf die fünf Punkte aus der ‚General information' im Text.

★★ **B** Sagen Sie auf Englisch, warum jeder Schritt der oben beschriebenen Anweisungen wichtig ist.

★ **C** Sagen Sie auf Deutsch, warum jeder Schritt der oben beschriebenen Anweisungen wichtig ist.

2 | Making an emergency call

1/36

A Sie rufen den Notdienst an. Sie sind noch ein bisschen zittrig, aber Sie müssen trotzdem in der Lage sein, die Fragen der Notrufzentrale zu verstehen. Suchen Sie die Fragen im Text ‚Calling the emergency hotline'. Hören Sie das Telefonat, um Ihre Antworten zu überprüfen.

Operator: …[1] ?
Caller: The floor is covered in oil. One of the cooks has slipped on it.
Operator: …[2] ?

Caller:	The restaurant 'Yummy Kitchen' at 999 Excitement Street.
Operator:	...³ ?
Caller:	A cook is bleeding quite badly.
Operator:	...⁴ ?
Caller:	Just one, luckily.

B   **Üben Sie mit einem Partner weitere Anrufe beim Notdienst in den folgenden Situationen. Wechseln Sie sich mit den Rollen des Anrufers und der Notrufzentrale ab.**

What happened	Where	Injuries			
has hurt hand on a machine	in the factory of 'Besterman' at 112 Lucky Road	1 person			
has fallen from a ladder	in the warehouse of 'SonnenPower' at the corner of Dropdown Street and 4th Avenue.	1 person			
has been a car accident	on the company road of the company 'AutoElektra'	2 people	1 person		
have got an electric shock	outdoors, in the car park at 'Intertec', 911 Sunnyside Street	1 person	2 people	1 person	

REMEMBER

He/she is (not) breathing.
They are (not) breathing.

THE SITUATION You work in the Health & Safety department of a company. Your boss has sent you the following e-mail.

Dear …

It is time for our company to do our yearly safety check-up. Would you please go through all the departments in the company and check if there are any potential hazards? If you find any hazards, you have to do the following things right away. Order a warning sign for that area. You can order them from CompanySigns.com. Also put up a sign—you can write it yourself—for that area right away, before someone gets hurt.

When you are finished, would you please write me a short report? I am looking forward to reading it.

Thanks and best regards
A. Grimm

1 Understanding instructions from an employer

Lesen Sie die E-Mail. Welche vier Dinge sollen Sie tun, und warum?

2 Describing dangers

A Sie gehen in Ihrer Firma von Abteilung zu Abteilung und finden jede Menge mögliche Gefahren. Sie machen Fotos mit Ihrem Handy (1–8). Wählen Sie für jedes Foto ein Schild (a–l) auf S. 71 aus, das Sie auf der Webseite bestellen können, und schreiben Sie einen Text für ein vorläufiges Schild auf ein Blatt Papier, wie im Beispiel. Verwenden Sie Ausdrücke aus der ‚Useful language'-Box.

Keep hands away from machine!

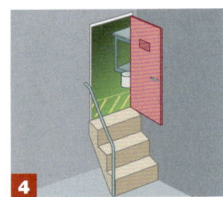

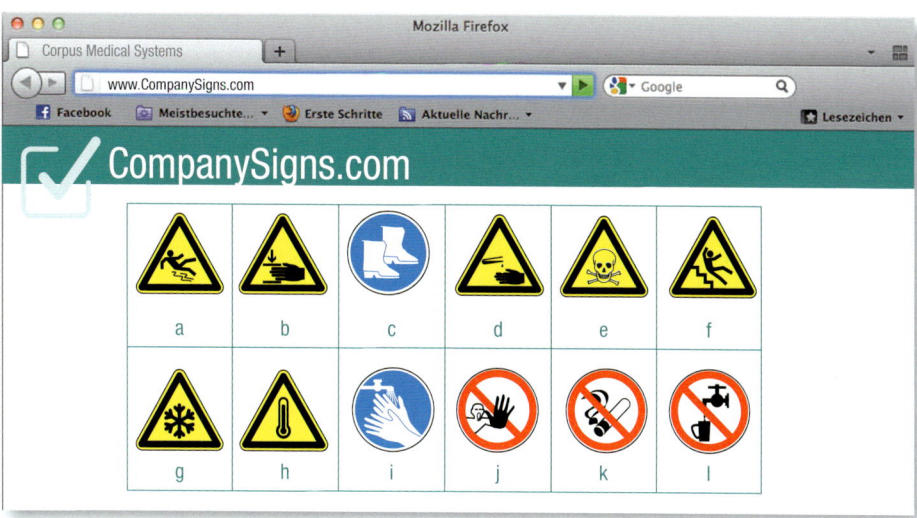

USEFUL LANGUAGE

Mind the … ! / Watch out for the … !	Vorsicht vor … ! / Achtung bei … !
Caution: … !	Achtung, … !
Keep hands/skin away from … !	Hände/Haut von … fern halten!
(Please,) No -ing!	(Bitte) Nicht … -en!
Do not … !	Nicht … !
chemicals	Chemikalien
enter	eintreten/betreten
high temperatures	hohe Temperaturen
poison	Gift
snow and ice	Schnee und Eis
steps	Stufen
wash	waschen
wear	tragen (Kleidung)
wet	nass

✈ **B** Notieren Sie die jeweilige Bedeutung der anderen Schilder von der Webseite. Verwenden Sie Ausdrücke aus der ‚Useful language'-Box.

3 | **Writing a report**

Schreiben Sie eine E-Mail an den Leiter der Arbeitssicherheit, in der Sie ihm schildern, welche Maßnahmen Sie ergriffen haben. Der Anfang der E-Mail ist bereits für Sie geschrieben.

Dear Mr Grimm

As you requested in your e-mail, I have found ten situations we need to pay attention to.

1. I saw an employee put his hand in a machine. Someone's hand could get hurt here.
2. There are some steps behind a door. Someone could fall here.
3. …

I have already … . I have also …

THE SITUATION You are attending a meeting for safety at work. There are people who do different types of work at the meeting.

1 Understanding safety hazards

A An der Sitzung nehmen Mitarbeiter mit den folgenden Jobs teil. Finden Sie für jeden das passende Foto an seinem jeweiligen Arbeitsplatz.

1 farm worker
2 shopkeeper
3 construction worker
4 IT worker
5 hairdresser
6 health care worker

a   b   c   d   e   f

1/37

B Fünf der oben genannten Teilnehmer drücken Ihre Sorge über Sicherheitsrisiken in ihren Jobs aus. Schreiben Sie, während Sie zuhören, die Reihenfolge auf, in der sie sprechen.

C Der Vorsitzende hat Sie gebeten, sich über die folgenden fünf Gefahrenkategorien zu informieren und ihm einige typische Jobs zu nennen, auf die die Kategorien zutreffen könnten. Wenn Sie für diese Übung Hilfe brauchen, können Sie auf der letzten Seite des Buches nachschauen.

		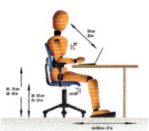		
Biological hazards come from bacteria and viruses.	Chemical hazards come from hazardous substances and fumes.	Ergonomic hazards come from uncomfortable chairs and workstations.	Physical hazards come from dangerous machines, noise, vibration, extreme light and temperatures.	Psychological hazards come from difficult schedules, unhappy customers, too many work hours and other forms of stress.

dangerous   gefährlich
fumes   Dämpfe
hazard   Gefahr
substance   Stoff
uncomfortable   unbequem

D   Der Vorsitzende hat die Teilnehmer gebeten, zuzuordnen, welche Jobs (aus Übung 1A-B) welchen Arten von Risiko ausgesetzt sind. Kopieren Sie die Tabelle unten. Hören Sie noch einmal die Sprecher 1–5 und kreuzen Sie jeweils das Kästchen mit der von ihnen genannten möglichen Gefahr an.

	Job	Biological	Chemical	Ergo-nomic	Physical	Psycho-logical
1	IT worker			x		

E   Überlegen Sie sich noch andere Gefahren, über die sich die Sprecher Sorgen machen sollten. Kreuzen Sie die entsprechenden Kästchen in Ihrer Tabelle an.

2 | Making safety recommendations

1/38

A   Hören Sie, wie der Vorsitzende den fünf Sprechern, die Sie in 1A gehört haben, Empfehlungen gibt. Stellen Sie für jede Empfehlung 1–5 fest, an wen sie gerichtet ist (den Landarbeiter, den IT-Angestellten etc.).

B   Setzen Sie die Sitzung in Ihrer Klasse fort. Geben Sie den Sprechern noch weitere Empfehlungen. Verwenden Sie dazu Ausdrücke aus der ‚Useful language'-Box.

USEFUL LANGUAGE
This person needs to …
This person should …
wear protective clothing (gloves, mask, boots, hard hat) — *Schutzkleidung tragen (Handschuhe, Maske, Stiefel, Schutzhelm)*
wear ear/eye protection — *Ohren-/Augenschutz tragen*
keep his/her … clean. Wash … — *seine/ihre … sauber halten. … waschen.*
open a window — *ein Fenster öffnen*
be careful when he/she … — *vorsichtig sein, wenn er/sie …*
inform himself/herself about … — *sich über … informieren*
ask his/her boss to … — *seinen/ihren Chef um … bitten*
get a better … — *sich eine/-n bessere/-n … besorgen*
take some days off — *ein paar Tage Urlaub nehmen*
take a break — *eine Pause machen*
work fewer hours — *kürzer arbeiten*

C   Sprechen Sie in einer Gruppe über die Sicherheitsgefahren, die Ihnen in Ihrem Beruf begegnen oder eines Tages begegnen könnten. Sprechen Sie auch Empfehlungen für diese Gefahren aus. Präsentieren Sie Ihre Ergebnisse in der Klasse.

Lerntipp

Klebezettel

Um zu lernen, wie Gegenstände heißen, sind Klebezettel ein geniales Hilfsmittel. Beschränken Sie sich dabei nicht auf Hauptwörter. Man kann mit Klebezetteln auch Adjektive lernen, z.B. *pretty*, *dirty* usw. Manchen macht es Spaß, die eigene Wohnung komplett zu beschriften. Um sich zu testen, nehmen Sie dann alle Zettel ab und versuchen Sie, sie wieder an die richtigen Stellen zu kleben.

Test

Sie haben die folgenden Klebezettel beschriftet. Wo sollen sie im Raum hingeklebt werden? Suchen Sie für jeden Klebezettel (1–16) die passende Stelle (a–p) auf den Bildern.

1 (p. 58)
paper tray

2 (p. 58)
'start' button

3 (p. 58)
display

4 (p. 58)
cover

5 (p. 60)
oven

6 (p. 60)
bowl

7 (p. 60)
pan

8 (p. 60)
plate

9 (p. 62)
screwdriver

10 (p. 62)
drill

11 (p. 62)
wood

12 (p. 63)
hammer

13 (p. 64)
workbench

14 (p. 65)
empty

15 (p. 67)
short

16 (p. 80)
uncomfortable

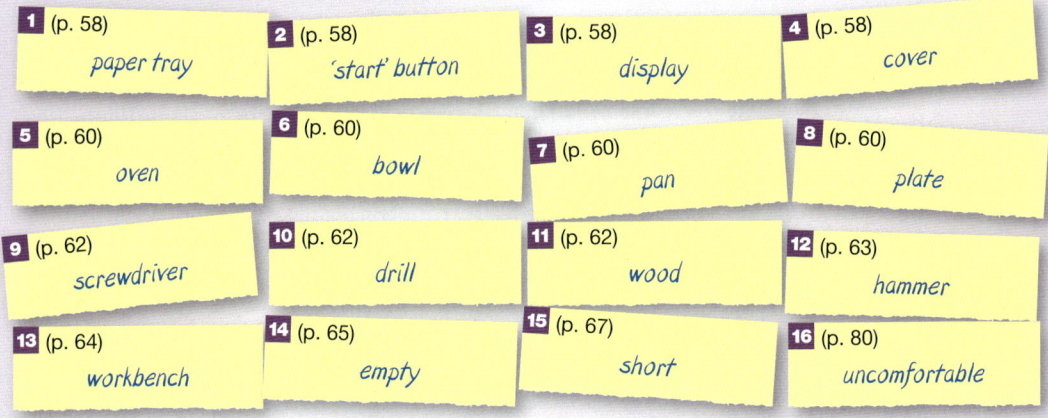

WEB CODE

Weitere Anregungen zum Vokabeltraining bekommen Sie, wenn Sie auf Cornelsen.de folgenden Webcode eingeben: **JBvocab4**

Mediation

ALLGEMEINE INFORMATIONEN ZUM PRÜFUNGSTEIL

Dieser Prüfungsteil macht 30 % der Punktwerte der schriftlichen Prüfung aus. Hier müssen Sie zeigen, dass Sie in der Lage sind, englische Sachtexte unter einer bestimmten Fragestellung auf Deutsch zu bearbeiten. Sie dürfen dabei ein zweisprachiges Wörterbuch benutzen – schlagen Sie jedoch nicht zu häufig nach, denn sonst verlieren Sie wertvolle Zeit. Verwenden Sie das Wörterbuch nur dann, wenn Sie die Bedeutung eines Wortes nicht dem Sinn nach erschließen können. Achten Sie bei der Lösung auch auf deutsche Sprachrichtigkeit, denn die Brauchbarkeit des Gesamtergebnisses wird in der Benotung berücksichtigt. Nehmen Sie sich für diese Aufgabe etwa 15 Minuten Zeit.

In Ihrer Firma wird gewünscht, dass man während der Ausbildung ein Praktikum im Ausland absolviert. Um die Bewerbungschancen für einen Praktikumsplatz in den USA zu erhöhen, hat man Sie damit beauftragt, auf Grundlage des folgenden Textes die wichtigsten Bewerbungstipps auf Deutsch in einem Informationsblatt für die Auszubildenden in Ihrer Firma zusammenzustellen. Sortieren Sie hierfür die entnommenen Informationen in einer Liste mit den fünf wichtigsten Dos und Don'ts.

How to **survive** a **job interview**
successfully!

Job interviews are a difficult thing – even more so when they take place in another country and when you have to talk in a foreign language. Often there are different rules. What is acceptable in your own country can be absolutely wrong in another country and the other way round.

Here are some tips that will help you through a job interview if you apply for a job in the USA:
- Employers often ask the same questions. Go online and look for what they typically ask and what the best answers are. Then practise the job interview with a friend.
- The employer will probably ask you what your talents are. Think about this before the interview and have an answer ready. If you did something successfully, talk about it!
- Your future employer will not hire you if you don't know anything about the company you apply to. When the question comes up, 'Why did you apply for a job in our company?' you must have a good answer. And don't tell them that you sent applications to other companies, too! You should make your potential employers think that you only want to work for their company!
- Remember the interviewer's name and use it during the interview. This makes the conversation more personal and it also shows your interest in the company and its staff.
- Make sure you are dressed correctly. Wear nice, professional clothes. Don't put on too much make-up or jewellery. Don't use too much perfume or aftershave, either.
- Don't forget to take a pen and paper for note-taking with you.
- Be on time for the interview. 'On time' means five to ten minutes early. If necessary, go to the company a few days before the interview, so you know how long it will take to get there.
- During the job interview, try to relax. But don't be too relaxed! Sit properly on your chair and concentrate.
- Keep eye contact with the interviewer. Pay attention to what he or she says. Listen to the entire question before you answer it. Don't talk too long when you answer a question.
- When you discuss your education and job experiences, try to match them with what the company is looking for.
- When they ask you about your hobbies, don't talk about them for too long. If you have done some volunteer work, then talk about it!
- Send a thank-you note after the interview and say that you are still interested in the position.

THE SITUATION Samira Polat works for a big department store, and she is an assistant to buyer Helga Grasse. Helga often sees international sales representatives and uses English more than German, so Samira keeps Helga's diary in English.

⏱	Monday, January 21st	Tuesday, January 22nd
8.30	Meeting with purchasing staff	
9.00		IT systems meeting
9.30		
10.00	E-mails & phone calls	
10.30		E-mails & phone calls
11.00		
11.30	Meeting with Household Goods Floor Manager	
12.00		See Orient Carpets rep.
12.30		Fitness studio
1.00		
1.30	Lunch with Director	Lunch with friends
2.00	See Living Luxury rep.	
2.30		Meeting with sales team
3.00		
3.30	Visit warehouse	
4.00		
4.30		
5.00		See Kitchen King rep.
5.30		

floor manager — Abteilungsleiter
purchasing — Einkauf
sales representative (rep.) — Vertreter

1 Talking about appointments

A Machen Sie sich mit dem Terminkalender vertraut und beantworten Sie die Fragen.

1 How many appointments with reps. does Helga have on Monday and Tuesday?
2 How much time does she usually give to a rep.?
3 Which colleagues is Helga going to meet during Monday and Tuesday?
4 When does she have time for any more appointments?

B Arbeiten Sie mit einem Partner und nehmen Sie die Rollen von Helga und Samira ein. Stellen und beantworten Sie Fragen wie diese.

Helga What time am I having my meeting with the purchasing staff on Monday?
Samira From 8.30 to 9.00.
Helga When am I going to lunch with the Director?
Samira At 1.00.

> ### REMEMBER
>
> **Für Dinge, die jetzt passieren:**
> *What are you doing at the moment? I'm studying English.*
> **Für zukünftige Pläne und Vereinbarungen (ähnlich wie die Zukunft mit *going to*):**
> *What are you doing tomorrow? I'm travelling to Paris.*

2 | Asking for an appointment

KMK

A   Lesen Sie die E-Mail und beantworten Sie die Fragen auf Deutsch.

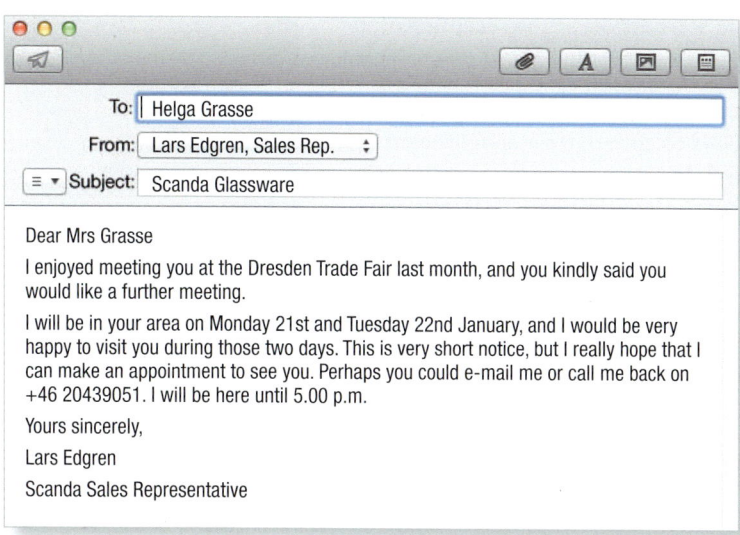

To: | Helga Grasse
From: | Lars Edgren, Sales Rep.
Subject: | Scanda Glassware

Dear Mrs Grasse

I enjoyed meeting you at the Dresden Trade Fair last month, and you kindly said you would like a further meeting.

I will be in your area on Monday 21st and Tuesday 22nd January, and I would be very happy to visit you during those two days. This is very short notice, but I really hope that I can make an appointment to see you. Perhaps you could e-mail me or call me back on +46 20439051. I will be here until 5.00 p.m.

Yours sincerely,

Lars Edgren

Scanda Sales Representative

1   Wer ist Lars Edgren?
2   Woher kennt er Helga Grasse?
3   Was ist das Problem mit Lars Edgrens Anliegen?
4   Was glauben Sie, warum Helga trotzdem froh sein könnte ihn, zu treffen?
5   Wie und bis wann kann Helga Lars Edgren erreichen?

B   Schreiben Sie eine E-Mail auf Englisch von Helga Grasse an Lars Edgren, in der Sie ihm mitteilen, dass sich Ihre Assistentin, Samira Polat, mit ihm in Verbindung setzen und einen Termin vereinbaren wird.

3 | Making appointments

2/1

A   Hören Sie sich das Telefongespräch zwischen Samira und Lars Edgren an. Notieren Sie Datum und Uhrzeit von Lars Edgrens Termin mit Helga Grasse.

YOUR CHOICE

★

B   Vereinbaren Sie mit einem Partner einen Termin, um einander zu treffen. Partner A verwendet File 15 auf S. 140, Partner B verwendet File 17 auf S. 141.

★★

C   Vereinbaren Sie mit einem Partner einen Termin, um einander zu treffen. Partner A verwendet File 16 auf S. 140, Partner B verwendet File 18 auf S. 141.

USEFUL LANGUAGE	Questions	Answers
	Can I make an appointment?	My only free time is from … to …
	Can you see me on …?	I'm sorry, but I can't make it on …
	What about …?	That's perfect for me!
	Could you e-mail or call me back on …?	I'll call you / send you an e-mail to confirm the appointment.

THE SITUATION

Monica Stern works at the reception of a doctor's surgery with a lot of non-German patients. As a result, she often needs to speak in English. Here she is helping people who need to change their appointments to a later date.

Mittwoch 2. Juni			Donnerstag 3. Juni		
Uhr-zeit	Dr Khan	Krankenschwester Blek	Uhr-zeit	Dr Khan	Krankenschwester Blek
16:10	Brandt, Peter	Nilsen, Jens	9:00	Hart, Steffi	
16:20	Carter, Julia	Krenz, Gaby	9:10		
16:30	Harmel, Paul	Nowak, Ewa	9:20	Pertini, Paulo	Guzman, Anna
16:40	Blanc, Marie	Harmel, Paul	9:30		

1 Changing appointments

2/2

A Suchen Sie die Termine von Herrn Harmel oben in der Liste. Hören Sie sich dann sein Gespräch mit Monica Stern an und notieren Sie das Datum und die Uhrzeit seiner beiden neuen Termine.

B Lesen Sie den Dialog und ordnen Sie die deutschen Formulierungen (1–5) denen zu, die Monica Stern verwendet.

Ms Stern	Good afternoon, Mr Harmel. How can I help you?
Mr Harmel	I'm calling about tomorrow afternoon's appointments.
Ms Stern	Ah, yes. You're seeing the doctor at 4.30, and then you're seeing the nurse at 4.40. Is there a problem?
Mr Harmel	Yes, there is. I'm very sorry, but I can't get to you then. Have you got any other appointments after 5.00?
Ms Stern	I'm sorry, but there aren't any more.
Mr Harmel	What about the day after tomorrow? Is there anything available?
Ms Stern	Yes, there are still one or two available.
Mr Harmel	Good! What sort of times have you got?
Ms Stern	I can give you an appointment with the nurse at 9.00.
Mr Harmel	That sounds good.
Ms Stern	And you can have an appointment with the doctor at 9.10.
Mr Harmel	That's perfect for me. Thank you.
Ms Stern	You're very welcome.

1 ‚Ich kann Ihnen einen Termin bei der Schwester um 9:00 Uhr geben.'
2 ‚Es tut mir leid, aber es sind keine mehr frei.'
3 ‚Gibt es ein Problem?'
4 ‚Und Sie können einen Termin beim Doktor um 9:10 Uhr bekommen.'
5 ‚Ja, es sind noch einer oder zwei verfügbar.'

C Nehmen Sie mit einem Partner die Rollen von Monica Stern und einem Patienten ein und verschieben Sie einen Termin. Verwenden Sie dazu die Terminliste oben.

D Partnerarbeit: Erstellen Sie eine Terminliste für die kommenden zwei Tage. Rufen Sie sich dann abwechselnd gegenseitig an, um einen Termin zu verschieben.

NEW SITUATION Max Kellner is a receptionist at a tourist hotel. He often has to use English with his guests. At the moment he is dealing with people who need to change their reservations.

2 | Changing reservations

A Ordnen Sie die deutschen Wörter in der Reservierungsliste den folgenden englischen Wörtern (a–f) zu.

a accommodation   **c** booking date   **e** reservations
b availability   **d** double room   **f** single room

Reservierungen					
Name	Buchungsdatum				Unterbringung
Juni	4	5	6	7	
Brady, Susan	DZ	DZ	DZ	DZ	2 Doppelzimmer
Le Clerc, Denise			EZ		1 Einzelzimmer
Nordman, Tim				EZ	1 Einzelzimmer

Verfügbarkeit			
Juni	12	13	14
Einzelzimmer	2	0	1
Doppelzimmer	2	1	2
Familienzimmer	1	2	0

2/3

B Hören Sie zu und notieren Sie den Namen des Gastes und die Details der veränderten Reservierung.

C Hören Sie sich das Gespräch erneut an und beantworten Sie die Fragen.

1 How can you ask if everything is OK?
2 What can you say to check what someone means?
3 How can you say that the same rooms are not available?
4 What can you say to offer an alternative?
5 How do you reply politely to someone's thanks?

D Partnerarbeit: Nehmen Sie die Rollen von Max Kellner und Tim Normani ein, der seine Reservierung vom 7. Juni auf den 14. Juni verschieben muss. Zudem benötigt er nun ein Doppelzimmer, da seine Frau ihn begleiten wird.

E Führen Sie mit Hilfe der folgenden Vorgaben ein Rollenspiel durch, in dem ein Kunde an Ihrem Arbeitsplatz anruft und einen Termin verschieben will.

KMK

Angestellter

Fragen Sie, ob Ihr Termin für nächste Woche in Ordnung geht.

Kunde

Entschuldigen Sie sich und sagen Sie, dass Sie den Termin leider verschieben müssen. Bitten Sie um einen späteren Termin.

Bieten Sie eine andere Tageszeit an.

Stimmen Sie zu und bedanken Sie sich.

Wiederholen Sie den neuen Termin und verabschieden Sie sich.

Verabschieden Sie sich.

THE SITUATION You work for the company SonnenPower in Stuttgart. You and your colleagues are expecting a team from Prague in the Czech Republic, but they are running late. They send you text messages in English, which you have to translate for your colleagues.

1 Mediating information about delays

A Lesen Sie die SMS (A–E) und bringen Sie sie in die auf der Karte gekennzeichnete Reihenfolge (1–5). Wann werden die Tschechen ankommen?

A Team aus Prag
Now at Czech-German border.

B Team aus Prag
Sorry, equipment arrived late. Leaving Prague now.

C Team aus Prag
50 kms to Stuttgart, should be with you in an hour.

D Team aus Prag
Car OK again, but now big traffic jam on motorway.

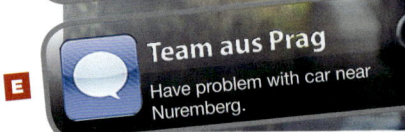

E Team aus Prag
Have problem with car near Nuremberg.

B Mit jeder neuen SMS, die auf Ihrem Handy ankommt, müssen Sie Ihre Kollegen auf den neuesten Stand bringen. Informieren Sie die Kollegen nach jeder SMS auf Deutsch.

1 *Sie schreiben, dass ihre Ausrüstung spät angekommen ist und sie jetzt erst aus Prag losfahren.*

2 *...*

2 | Writing text messages

A Machen Sie aus den SMS auf S. 80 komplette Sätze. Verwenden Sie diese Wörter.

> a • a • ~~our~~ • is • It's • so we • The • the • the • the • there is • We • ~~We are~~ • We are

1 *Sorry, our equipment arrived late. We are leaving Prague now.*
2 ...

B Die Tschechen verspäten sich im Stadtverkehr noch mehr. Sie sollen deshalb nun direkt zu einer Baustelle in der Gredinger Str. 15 kommen (ein Navi haben sie an Bord). Teilen Sie ihnen dies mit, indem Sie ihnen eine SMS auf Englisch schreiben.

C Wenn Sie Ihren Geschäftspartner gut kennen, können Sie in Ihren SMS auch Abkürzungen verwenden. Notieren Sie zu den Abkürzungen (1–7) die entsprechenden Bedeutungen auf Englisch. Schreiben Sie dann eine SMS, in der Sie möglichst viele Abkürzungen verwenden.

1 pls   *please*
2 thx
3 4u
4 @
5 2
6 B
7 cu

REMEMBER		
You	**will be**	late.
He/She/It	**won't arrive**	on time.

3 | Understanding information about delays   KMK

NEW SITUATION Sie haben eine Tagung mit mehr als 20 Teilnehmern organisiert, darunter sind Maria Largo, Etienne Retard, Benjamin Turtle, Ania Wolna und Mirek Šnek. Es ist der Morgen der Veranstaltung und die Teilnehmer werden um 11 Uhr erwartet.

2/4

A Sie haben fünf Nachrichten auf Ihrem Anrufbeantworter. Machen Sie sich Notizen, damit Sie Ihre Kollegen über den neuesten Stand informieren können. Die wichtigsten Informationen sind der Name des Anrufers und wann er eintreffen wird.

B Schicken Sie Ihrem Kollegen David Parker eine kurze E-Mail auf Englisch und geben Sie ihm die Informationen aus 3A durch. Teilen Sie ihm mit, dass Sie sich selbst auch um eine Viertelstunde verspäten werden.

THE SITUATION — Jürgen Schmidt of TotalTech GmbH wants to import and sell a new 3D printer from the Japanese company Ichiban Optics. In just minutes, these amazing printers turn a 3D design on a computer into a solid 3D object.

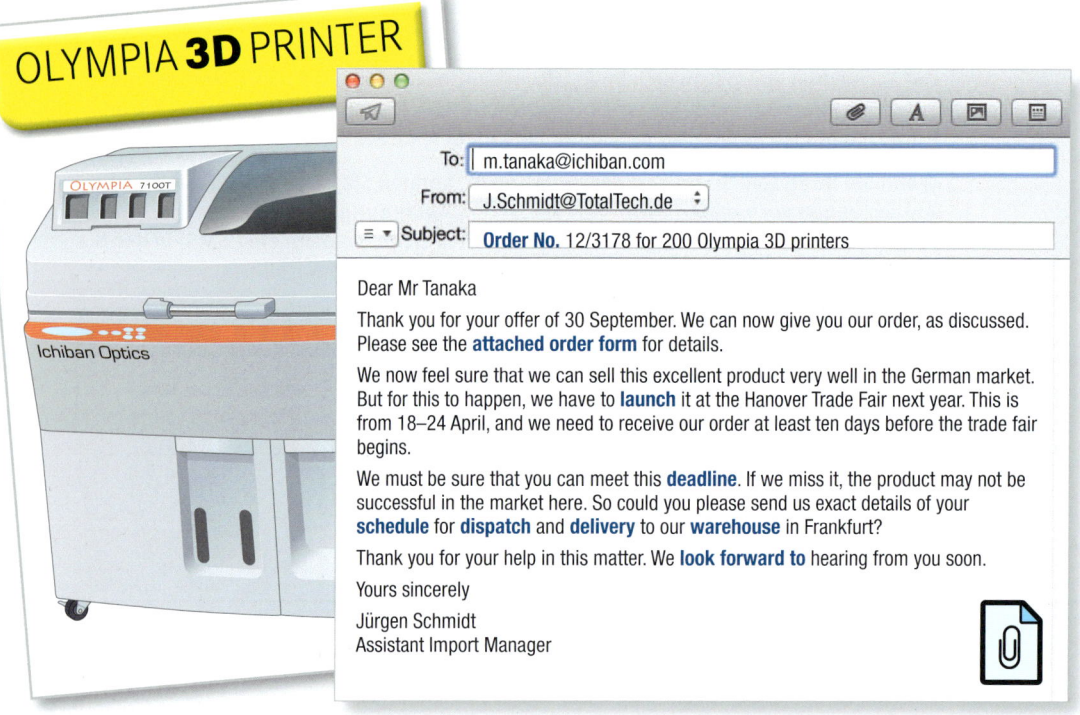

OLYMPIA **3D** PRINTER

OLYMPIA 7100T

Ichiban Optics

To: m.tanaka@ichiban.com
From: J.Schmidt@TotalTech.de
Subject: **Order No.** 12/3178 for 200 Olympia 3D printers

Dear Mr Tanaka

Thank you for your offer of 30 September. We can now give you our order, as discussed. Please see the **attached order form** for details.

We now feel sure that we can sell this excellent product very well in the German market. But for this to happen, we have to **launch** it at the Hanover Trade Fair next year. This is from 18–24 April, and we need to receive our order at least ten days before the trade fair begins.

We must be sure that you can meet this **deadline**. If we miss it, the product may not be successful in the market here. So could you please send us exact details of your **schedule** for **dispatch** and **delivery** to our **warehouse** in Frankfurt?

Thank you for your help in this matter. We **look forward to** hearing from you soon.

Yours sincerely

Jürgen Schmidt
Assistant Import Manager

1 | Ordering a product

A Beantworten Sie die Fragen zu Jürgen Schmidts E-Mail.

1 What is his e-mail responding to?
2 By when does Ichiban Optics have to deliver the order?
3 Why is the delivery date so important?

B Ordnen Sie die in der E-Mail blau hervorgehobenen Begriffe den folgenden deutschen Begriffen (1–10) zu.

1 Auftragsnummer	**5** (ein Produkt auf dem Markt) einführen	**8** Terminvorgabe
2 beigefügt		**9** Versand
3 Lagerhalle	**6** Bestellformular	**10** Zeitplan
4 Lieferung	**7** sich auf … freuen	

C Schreiben Sie eine E-Mail auf Englisch an die Vertriebsleiterin Karen Fielding und informieren Sie sie über die bestellten Drucker und deren geplante Markteinführung in Deutschland sowie die nächsten Schritte, die von Ichiban Optics gemacht werden sollen. Achten Sie auf die korrekte Form (Betreff, Anrede, Schlussformel). **KMK**

NEW SITUATION Mr Tanaka has replied with a schedule that gives TotalTech their order by 5 April. Everything seems to be going well, but then there is suddenly a big problem.

2 | Dealing with a delivery delay

A Lesen Sie die E-Mails (A–D) und bringen Sie sie in die richtige Reihenfolge. Begründen Sie Ihre Entscheidung.

A

Dear Mr Tanaka

We are very worried to hear about the situation in Thailand. If we miss the Hanover Trade Fair deadline, we will lose many sales. In this situation, we may have to put a stop on our order.

Is there anything you can do to help? We look forward to hearing from you very soon.

Best regards

Jürgen Schmidt

Dear Mr Tanaka

Thank you very much for your last e-mail. We were very happy to hear that the situation has improved. We have discussed your plan and are happy to accept it.

Kind regards

B Jürgen Schmidt

C

Dear Mr Schmidt

We are very sorry to hear that you may cancel Order No. 12/3178. We want to do everything possible to keep it.

Luckily, we have some good news from Thailand. Production is starting again, and so we can complete your order by 26 March. We want to make you this offer: At our cost, we will dispatch part of the order by air to reach you by 7 April. We offer to send 10 % in this way. The rest can follow by sea, and this will reach you by about 15 May.

We think this will meet your needs at Hanover and look forward to hearing from you.

Best wishes

Mitsuo Tanaka

Dear Mr Schmidt

You must know from the news about the terrible floods in Thailand. Like many Japanese companies, we have a factory there and it is under water. As it produces parts for the Olympia 3D printers, we probably cannot deliver the products to you on time.

We are very sorry about this. I will contact you again as soon as I have more information.

Best wishes

Mitsuo Tanaka

D

B Lesen Sie die E-Mails noch einmal und beantworten Sie die Fragen.

1 Wie können Sie sagen, dass es Ihnen leid tut, schlechte Nachrichten zu überbringen?
2 Wie können Sie auf schlechte Nachrichten antworten?
3 Wie können Sie gute Neuigkeiten ankündigen?
4 Wie können Sie auf gute Neuigkeiten antworten?
5 Wie können Sie eine E-Mail beenden, auf die Sie sich eine schnelle Antwort erhoffen?
6 Welche Schlussformeln verwenden die beiden Verfasser der E-Mails?

C Schreiben Sie eine E-Mail auf Englisch an Karen Fielding mit den guten Neuigkeiten aus E-Mail C. Fragen Sie, ob sie mit dem Plan einverstanden ist, und bitten Sie um eine zügige Antwort.

D Nehmen Sie die Rolle von Karen Fielding ein und schreiben Sie eine Antwort auf Englisch. Reagieren Sie positiv auf die Neuigkeiten und das geplante Vorgehen.

Doing a work placement in the UK
12.1
Ein Praktikum in Großbritannien machen

THE SITUATION You are going to spend six months in Cardiff in Wales as a trainee.
To prepare yourself, you attend a seminar on working in the UK.

1   Finding places on a map

Zu Beginn des Seminars bekommen Sie eine Landkarte Großbritanniens und Irlands.
Finden Sie mit einem Partner die folgenden Länder und Städte auf der Karte.

Countries
- England
- Northern Ireland
- Republic of Ireland
- Scotland
- Wales

Cities
- Belfast
- Cardiff
- Dublin
- Edinburgh
- London

2   Understanding and mediating a talk

2/5

A   Hören Sie einen kurzen Vortrag über das Arbeitsleben in Großbritannien.
Beantworten Sie die Fragen.

1   What time do most people start and finish work in the UK?
2   How do employees in the UK usually address their boss?
3   How should you address your boss when you first meet him or her?
4   Is British working culture more direct or more indirect?
5   What can you say if you don't understand a person?

B   Hören Sie sich den Vortrag noch einmal an. Fassen Sie die wichtigsten
Informationen über die Arbeitszeiten, die Anredeformen und die Arbeitskultur auf
Deutsch zusammen.

USEFUL LANGUAGE	Questions	Answers
	Where in … do you come from?	I'm from … in the north/south/east/west.
	What's the capital city of …?	The capital city is …
	Are there any famous actors and singers where you come from?	We have lots of famous actors and singers, like …
	What is German/English food like?	The food is tasty. We often cook sausages/ potatoes/pasta.
	What (fun things) can you do in …?	You can go cycling/sightseeing/shopping. We have a cinema / two interesting museums / lots of bars and restaurants / mountains / a beautiful park in …

(NEW SITUATION) **You are now in Cardiff for your work placement. Your boss is Jeremy Pratt, and he is from Scotland.**

3 | Talking about where you come from

A Jeremy Pratt möchte mehr über Deutschland erfahren. Führen Sie mit einem Partner das folgende Gespräch. Verwenden Sie als Hilfe die ‚Useful language'-Box auf S. 84. Wechseln Sie anschließend die Rollen.

Jeremy Pratt

Ask where in Germany she/he comes from.

Trainee

Tell Jeremy where you are from.

Ask what the capital city is.

Say what the capital city is.

Are there any famous German actors/singers?

Name some famous German actors/singers.

What's German food like?

Describe German food.

What fun things can you do in your town ?

Talk about things you can do in your town.

✈ **B** Überlegen Sie sich drei weitere Fragen und setzen Sie das Gespräch fort.

C In Cardiff werden Ihnen die folgenden Fragen gestellt. Eine der Antworten ist förmlicher und sollte bei Vorgesetzten verwendet werden, die andere ist eher für Freunde geeignet. Wählen Sie die jeweils angemessene Antwort.

1 'Would you like a beer?'
   a 'No thanks, I hate beer.'
   b 'Thank you, but I prefer wine.'

2 'What do you think of Jeremy's plan?'
   a 'I think there's a problem with the plan.'
   b 'It's a terrible plan.'

3 'Is your workload OK?'
   a 'Aye, it's fine.'
   b 'Yes, thank you for asking.'

4 'Has the delivery arrived yet?'
   a 'No.'
   b 'I'm afraid the delivery is late.'

5 'Would you like some coffee?'
   a 'No, thank you.'
   b 'Maybe later.'

6 'Right?'
   a 'Hi.'
   b 'Good morning.'

7 'Here's the sandwich you wanted.'
   a 'Cheers.'
   b 'Thank you very much.'

CULTURE In Großbritannien wird manchmal auch Umgangssprache verwendet. Einige der häufigsten umgangssprachlichen Äußerungen sind z.B. *right = hello, good morning; aye = yes; cheers = thanks; fag = cigarette.*

THE SITUATION Kevin Rödiger works for Lotus Paper Inc., an American company with a branch in Germany. Many of his colleagues are American.

1 | Understanding cultural differences

A Lesen Sie den Text. Erstellen Sie für die neuen Auszubildenden von Lotus Paper Inc. ein Infoblatt auf Deutsch, in dem Sie die wichtigsten kulturellen Unterschiede stichpunktartig zusammenfassen.

KMK

You're hired!

Every country has its own culture, and these cultures can cause misunderstandings and problems. In Germany many American companies have set up branches, and the differences between American and German staff may surprise you if you are not prepared.

Something as simple as dates and numbers can be a problem. For example, in Germany, and all of Europe, 06.11. is the sixth of November. In the USA, it is the eleventh of June. When saying large numbers such as 3,500, Americans say thirty-five hundred, rather than three thousand five hundred. Also Americans use a twelve-hour clock, not a twenty-four hour clock like Germans.

In the USA, there are many laws to protect people of different ethnic backgrounds and gender against discrimination. Americans do not add a photo to their CV because an employer should not choose a candidate because of his or her appearance. Every employee in the USA must be treated the same, but men usually still earn more money for the same job than women, and it is harder for women to get promotions within a company.

In most American companies there is a dress code. If the company has a uniform, the employee must wear it, and in financial firms employees wear suits. In all other companies, the employee can wear what he or she likes, as long as it is not offensive.

In the USA employees and bosses use each other's first names, and many employees spend time together at the weekends and become friends.

Americans like to smile, joke and make small talk. These things are more important in an American company than in a German one. Americans have a reputation for being loud and direct, but this is not true. In American companies, people are usually polite. For example, if you want a person to do something for you, you should not say, 'Bring me a coffee!' Instead, you should say, 'Could you bring me a coffee, please?'

Americans also like to be on time for meetings, but if you are ten or fifteen minutes early or late, that's OK too. Meetings also often run later than planned.

"LET'S HEAR YOU TALK THE TALK... CAN YOU SAY 'NO' IN SPANISH, RUSSIAN, FRENCH, GERMAN, CHINESE, THAI...?"

discrimination	Benachteiligung
offensive	anstößig
promotion	Beförderung
treat	behandeln

B Entscheiden Sie, ob die Aussagen (1–8) eher auf die deutsche oder eher auf die amerikanische Geschäftskultur zutreffen. Manche Aussagen können zu beiden Kulturen gehören.

1 04.03. is the third of April.
2 Never arrive at a meeting late.
3 Many employees are friends.
4 The working culture is generally more indirect than direct.
5 Instructions should be put as questions.
6 Meetings must begin and end on time.
7 Before doing business, make small talk.
8 Employees usually call their boss by his or her first name.

2 | Expressing criticism and compliments

2/6

A Hören Sie sich das Gespräch über Kevins Arbeit an und beantworten Sie die Fragen.

1 Welche Komplimente macht die Chefin Kevin?
2 Welchen Fehler hat Kevin gemacht?
3 Warum ist Kevins Chefin verärgert?
4 Welche Anweisung gibt sie ihm für die Zukunft?

B Lesen Sie die ‚Culture'-Box und schreiben Sie ‚criticism sandwiches' für die folgenden Probleme.

1 An employee was rude to another employee.
2 An employee was late for work.
3 An employee's work is not good enough.

> **CULTURE**
>
> In der englischsprachigen Welt kritisieren Vorgesetzte ihre Angestellten oft in Form eines *criticism sandwich*. Der Chef beginnt damit, etwas Nettes zu sagen (z.B. *'You're doing a great job.'*), dann folgt ein Kritikpunkt (z.B. *'There's just one thing …'*) und zum Schluss kommt wieder etwas Nettes (z.B. *'We're very happy with your work.'*). Auf diese Weise ist die Kritik zwischen zwei Komplimenten eingebettet und besser ‚verdaulich'.

3 | Saying no

★ **A** In der amerikanischen Geschäftskultur sollten Sie Nein nur auf indirekte Weise sagen. Üben Sie dies in Partnerarbeit in den folgenden Situationen. Verwenden Sie als Hilfe die ‚Useful language'-Box.

1 Ihre Chefin fragt Sie, ob Sie heute länger arbeiten können.
2 Ein Bekannter fragt Sie, ob Sie heute Abend mit ihm in eine Bar gehen wollen.
3 Ihr Vorgesetzter fragt Sie, ob Sie am kommenden Wochenende arbeiten können.
4 Ein Kollege bittet Sie, Kaffee für die Kaffeemaschine an Ihrem Arbeitsplatz zu besorgen.

★★ **B** Partner A verwendet File 19 auf S. 142, Partner B verwendet File 21 auf S. 143. Spielen Sie die Situation durch.

> **USEFUL LANGUAGE**
>
> | Questions | Ways of saying no |
> |---|---|
> | Can you work late? | I'm afraid I don't have time. |
> | Would you like to go to a bar tonight? | I'm sorry, I'm too busy. |
> | Could you please buy some coffee? | I'm sorry, but I have another appointment. |
> | Can you work this weekend? | Sorry, I have to spend time with my family. |

THE SITUATION Your company so far has not had any business contacts with Chinese companies but would like to in the future. Your boss, Mrs Santos, asks you to do some research and you find the following information.

1 Understanding Chinese business culture

A Lesen Sie den Text und erstellen Sie eine Liste auf Englisch mit den wichtigsten Dos und Don'ts im Umgang mit chinesischen Geschäftspartnern.

TIPS FOR DOING BUSINESS WITH CHINA

1 Introductions and greetings

The Chinese way of greeting is a slight bow, but with Western partners the Chinese often shake hands. When you offer your business card to a Chinese partner, you should use both hands to hold it and bow a little.

Use the family name with the job title to address your business contact, for example, 'Manager Liu'. Do not use the first name, except when you are invited to do so. Do not put the business card in your pocket right away and do not make notes on the card in front of the person who gives it to you.

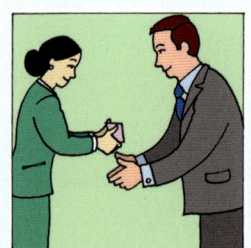

柳 静云
Liu Jingyun

PR China

Manager of Purchasing Department
Red Star Import and Export Company Ltd.
No. 138, Chezhan Rd, Furong District
410008 Changsha

Jingyun is the first name.

Liu is the family name.

bow	*sich verbeugen*
grave	*Grab*
host	*Gastgeber*

2 Business meetings

Usually the most important person comes into a room first. Meetings begin with small talk, and it is impolite to talk about business right away. Try to speak a few words in Chinese because this shows an interest in Chinese culture. Actually, this is always a good idea when you meet people from other countries.

3 Eating out

If you are invited to a formal dinner in China, your host will perhaps ask you to give a short speech. Often you sit around big round tables with different dishes on them. If the host serves food for you, you should accept it and show that you like the food. Do not refuse dishes, even if you do not like the food. Always leave something on your plate at the end of the meal or your host may think that you are still hungry and will order more food.

4 Giving presents

Something from your region is perfect as a present. Good packaging is important: red, green and golden colours are popular but plain black or white are colours for sadness. A present should be given with both hands, and it is polite to say that the present is only something small. In China people usually do not open the present right away. An umbrella is not a suitable present because its Chinese name sounds like 'breaking up'. Flowers are fine, but not chrysanthemums because people put them on graves.

B Schreiben Sie auf Deutsch eine E-Mail an Frau Santos und teilen Sie ihr mit, was Sie über die chinesische Geschäftskultur herausgefunden haben. Erklären Sie, welches Verhalten in verschiedenen Situation angemessen ist.

2 Doing a quiz

A Lösen Sie das Quiz und finden Sie die richtigen Antworten. Verwenden Sie den Text aus S. 88 als Hilfe.

China quiz

1 A Chinese partner offers you his business card. How do you take it?

a With your right hand. [☆]
b With your left hand. [☆]
c With both of your hands. [☆]
d With your open hand. [☆]

2 You receive the following business card. How do you address the person?

张 凌云

Zhang Lingyun
Production Director

Shengjia Sheetmetal Company Ltd.
No. 98A, Shengjia Rd
Shenzhen, Guangdong
PR China

a Director Lingyun. [☆]
b Mr Lingyun. [☆]
c Mr Zhang. [☆]
d Director Zhang. [☆]

3 You want to greet a Chinese person in a friendly way. What do you do?

a Bow as low as you can. [☆]
b Bow slightly and shake hands. [☆]
c Wave your hand. [☆]
d Fold your hands and bow. [☆]

4 Who is the most important person in a group of Chinese business people?

a The loudest person. [☆]
b The person wearing the best suit. [☆]
c The first person to enter a room. [☆]
d The last person to leave a room. [☆]

5 Which of these things is not a good present for a Chinese business partner?

a A picture book of Germany. [☆]
b A white umbrella. [☆]
c A set of knives made in Germany. [☆]
d Yellow roses. [☆]

6 Which colour should you not use for the packaging of your present?

a Black. [☆]
b Pink. [☆]
c Red. [☆]
d Green. [☆]

7 Your Chinese host serves you some food which you do not like. How do you react?

a You refuse it and cover your plate. [☆]
b You refuse it and say that you do not like this food. [☆]
c You accept it and leave it on the plate. [☆]
d You accept it and give it to someone else. [☆]

8 What do you say when you are giving a Chinese person a present?

a 'It's only something small. I hope you like it!' [☆]
b 'It's a very expensive present. I spent a lot of money on it!' [☆]
c 'It's a luxury brand from Europe. I'm sure you won't find it in China!' [☆]
d 'It's a very special present. It took me a long time to find it!' [☆]

B Vergleichen Sie Ihre Antworten mit einem Partner. Für jede richtige Antwort gibt es einen Punkt. Finden Sie heraus, wer die meisten Punkte hat.

Aa Vocabulary test and learning tip

Lerntipp

Vokabellernen mit Kärtchen

Um Vokabeln zu lernen, müssen Sie nicht stundenlang pauken. Hier ist eine Methode, die Sie während einer fünfminütigen Busfahrt verwenden können. Schreiben Sie die Wörter auf Kärtchen oder Papierzettel. Auf die eine Seite schreiben Sie das englische Wort. Auf die andere Seite schreiben Sie die deutsche Übersetzung oder eine Definition auf Englisch.

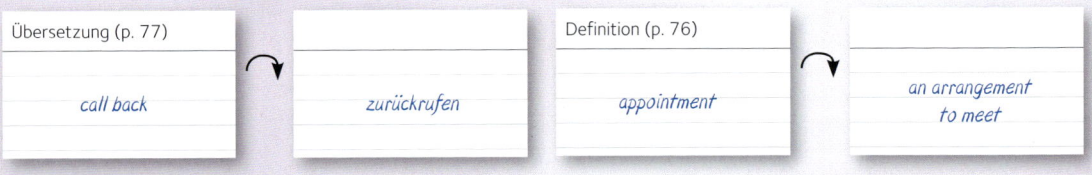

Übersetzung (p. 77)		Definition (p. 76)	
call back	zurückrufen	appointment	an arrangement to meet

Test

Vervollständigen Sie jedes Kärtchen mit dem passenden englischen oder deutschen Begriff. Schreiben Sie nicht in das Buch, sondern auf ein Blatt Papier oder auf Ihre eigenen Kärtchen.

Übersetzung (p. 76)		Übersetzung (p. 78)	
1 sale(s)	V...	**2** a...	verfügbar

Definition (p. 79)		Übersetzung (p. 80)	
3 a...	a place to spend the night	**4** traffic jam	S...

Übersetzung (p. 82)		Übersetzung (p. 85)	
5 s...	Zeitplan	**6** prefer	b...

Definition (p. 86)		Definition (p. 86)	
7 h...	give someone a job	**8** p...	something you give to someone (synonym: gift)

WEB CODE Wenn Sie noch nicht genug haben, sollten Sie ganz schnell auf Cornelsen.de gehen und den folgenden Webcode eingeben. **JBvocab5**

Interaktion

ALLGEMEINE INFORMATIONEN ZUM PRÜFUNGSTEIL

Der mündliche Teil der Prüfung wird in der Regel in einer Zweier- oder Gruppenprüfung durchgeführt. Im ersten Teil der Prüfung sprechen Sie z.B. über sich und Ihre Firma, Ihre Ausbildung, Ihre Pläne für die Zukunft oder ein berufsrelevantes Thema. Im zweiten Teil müssen Sie ein Rollenspiel gestalten; das kann z.B. ein Telefonat mit einem Kunden oder ein Gespräch mit einem Geschäftspartner sein. Die mündliche Prüfung dauert insgesamt 15 Minuten. Zusätzlich haben Sie normalerweise etwas Zeit zur Vorbereitung, bevor die eigentliche Prüfung beginnt. Wie lang die Vorbereitungszeit ist, hängt von der Art der Aufgaben ab und kann vom Prüfer bestimmt werden. In diesem Prüfungsteil können Sie maximal 30 Punkte erreichen. Zum Bestehen der gesamten Prüfung müssen Sie mindestens 15 Punkte erzielen.

1 Die folgenden Punkte dienen als Anregung zur Vorbereitung auf den ersten Teil der Prüfung. Am besten greifen Sie sich einige Punkte heraus und machen sich Notizen dazu. Achten Sie darauf, dass sich ein roter Faden durch das zieht, was Sie von sich und Ihrer Ausbildung erzählen. Bereiten Sie sich auf diesen Teil der Prüfung am besten mit einem Partner vor, indem Sie anhand Ihrer Notizen üben, möglichst frei zu sprechen.

1. Present your company:
   – What kind of company do you work for?
   – What does your company produce/sell?
   – Where is your company located?
   – How many people work there?
2. Talk about your training:
   – Do you like your training? Why/Why not?
   – In which departments have you worked?
   – What have you learned during your training?
   – What did you like best/least?
   – Do you enjoy going to vocational school?

3. Talk about your plans for the future:
   – Will you stay in your company?
   – Are you looking for a job? Where? How?
   – Do you have any special future plans?
4. Other possible topics:
   – Description of a product/service
   – Telephoning with a customer
   – Safety measures at work

2 Führen Sie ein Telefonat auf Englisch mit Ihrem Partner. Partner A verwendet File 20 auf S. 142, Partner B verwendet File 22 auf S. 143. Machen Sie sich mit der Situation auf Ihrer Rollenkarte vertraut und sehen Sie sich das Bestellformular genau an. Die Angaben auf den Rollenkarten dienen als Anregung für das Gespräch. Führen Sie ein möglichst freies Gespräch und gehen Sie auf die Aussagen Ihres Partners ein.

Getting a job

job advertisements | cover letters | CVs | interviews

Set-up

A   **Talk to your partner about getting a job. What do you think is the most difficult part? What's the easiest part?**

People often say that getting a job is hard. It's not. It's very easy to get a job. Getting a good job is hard! If you want to make burgers at Burger King, it is easy to get a job making burgers at Burger King. If you want to cook in an expensive restaurant, it's a little more difficult.
To get the job you want takes time. Luckily, all you have to do is follow these five steps, and you will get the perfect job for you.

1. Decide exactly what job you want.
You already know the field you want to work in. But what exactly do you want to do? What are you good at? What do you like? What don't you like?

2. Get the right qualifications.
Now that you know what job you want, it's time to get the qualifications. Go to college, a vocational school, an evening class, or even get the qualifications online. Work hard here, and getting a job later is easier.

3. Look for the right job.
This is the hardest part. There are many jobs, but only a few jobs are right for you. It can take a long time to find the right job – don't give up!

4. Apply for the job.
Write your CV, write a cover letter and send it to the company. Writing a good CV and cover letter takes time. Write it, check it, and then give it to a friend to check. If your CV and cover letter are no good, you will not get an interview.

5. Go to the interview.
Almost done! The interview is the last step, and the scariest. Be yourself. Be honest. The interviewer is probably the person you will work with, and he or she is thinking: 'Do I like this candidate? Can I work with him/her?'

The five steps to getting the perfect job are not really easy, but nothing that is good is ever easy. Be strong, be tough, and don't give up until you have the job you want. Good luck.

B   **Read the text and answer the following questions.**

1   What kind of job is difficult to get?
2   What ways can you get the qualifications you need?
3   When you apply for a job, what two things must you send to an employer?
4   How must you act in an interview?
5   Why does an interviewer ask the question: 'Do I like this candidate?'

SCENE 1 | **Applying for a job**

A   **Sie sind werdende/r Kfz-Mechaniker/in und suchen einen Job, der Ihnen sowohl Auslandserfahrung als auch neue Erfahrungen mit Kfz-Technik bringt. Am liebsten wollen Sie direkt in einer Werkstatt *(workshop)* arbeiten. Lesen Sie die Anzeige und entscheiden Sie, ob die nachfolgenden Aussagen richtig oder falsch sind und begründen Sie dies auf Deutsch. Beantworten Sie die Fragen in kurzen Stichworten auf Deutsch.**

Aussagen

1   Die Stellenanzeige entspricht den persönlichen Erwartungen, die oben genannt sind.
2   Für den Job bei Centr'Auto braucht man keine Berufserfahrung.
3   Die Firma kommt offenbar bis jetzt mit ihren Deutsch sprechenden Kunden klar.
4   Man muss Französisch sprechen können, um diesen Job zu bekommen.

Fragen

5   Was genau muss man in diesem Job tun?
6   Welche persönliche Eigenschaften sollte der Bewerber haben?
7   Wie bewirbt man sich um diese Stelle?

Junior Workshop Assistant

Centr'Auto in Belgium is hiring a new Junior Workshop Assistant.

Duties:
Help the whole workshop team.
Use the machines in the workshop.
Any other duties that are necessary.

You are young and responsible and you like working in a noisy workshop. Some experience necessary, but we will also train you. You must speak English and German. We speak English but we need someone who can deal with our German-speaking customers.

Please send a CV and cover letter to: Centr'Auto
Rue de Courtrai 32
6700 Arlon
Belgium

SCENARIO A

B Here is a cover letter for the job at Centr'Auto. Read the letter and answer the questions. Notice how Andreas uses the information from the job advert in his cover letter.

1 What are Andreas's qualifications?
2 What personal qualities does Andreas mention?
3 What experience does he talk about?
4 What documents has Andreas sent along with this letter?
5 How can Centr'Auto contact Andreas? Name three possibilities.

Andreas Mann
Prinzenstraße 12
99345 Erfurt
Germany
Tel: 0361 2648 5671
E-mail: andy.mann89@gmz.de

Centr'Auto
Rue de Courtrai 32
6700 Arlon
Belgium

31 March 2016

Dear Sir or Madam

Application: Junior Workshop Assistant

I would like to apply for the job of Junior Workshop Assistant. I am 18 years old and I have a ninth grade school leaving certificate, plus a qualification in auto mechanics from a vocational school. I have also done a three-year apprenticeship at a workshop here in Germany. I am a hard worker and I enjoy working with machines. My father repairs cars and I sometimes help him. I like noisy work, and I like working with my hands. I am a responsible person and I like working in a team. I also enjoy dealing with customers.

Please find enclosed a copy of my Europass CV. I look forward to hearing from you.

Yours faithfully

Andreas Mann

Andreas Mann

Enclosures

C When writing a cover letter, it's important to name some personal qualities that are relevant to the job. Which list of personal qualities (1–5) are relevant to which professional group (a–e)?

Business and commercial sector workers

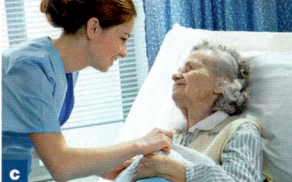
Health and care workers

Hotel and gastronomy workers

Technical workers

All professional groups

1
- polite
- hard-working
- flexible
- responsible
- interested in the job
- have specialized knowledge
- have good communication skills
- willing to take criticism and learn
- like/enjoy working with …

2
- good with hands
- independent
- like noisy workspaces
- have an eye for details
- able to think analytically
- can work quickly but carefully

3
- friendly
- interested in customer service
- creative in the kitchen
- a good memory
- physically fit
- able to deal with busy and slow periods
- flexible, willing to work weekends, evenings and holidays

4
- caring, have empathy for patients/residents
- interested in patients'/ residents' well-being
- physically fit, able to lift and move people
- able to deal with psychological stress
- organized
- flexible, able to work different shifts

5
- organized
- good with words, languages and communication
- customer-oriented but also company-oriented
- knowledge of Word, Excel and PowerPoint
- able to sit for long periods of time
- a team worker

D What personal qualities do you need for your job? Tell a partner.

E Write a cover letter for a job you would like to have. Use Andreas's cover letter from exercise B to help you. Include the skills from exercises C and D, and don't forget the proper beginning and end (Dear… / Yours faithfully).

95

SCENE 2 **Writing a CV**

YOUNGPROS.COM

Now streaming live:
Job Coach Francois Duchamps
explains the Europass CV.

Listen now →

2/7

A Listen to the interview about the Europass CV and say whether the following statements are true or false. Rewrite the false statements.

1 The Europass CV is a CV that you can use in the entire European Union.
2 The information on the Europass CV is the same as on a normal CV.
3 The Language Passport teaches an employer how to speak another language.
4 You can download a Europass CV from the website.
5 You can only post the Europass CV to an employer.

B Listen again and write down three reasons why the Europass CV is good.

C Mr Duchamps names seven types of information that should be on a CV. Listen again and write them down.

D Read the CV on p. 154–155 and answer the following questions.

1 Can you see on the CV what job Robert is applying for?
2 Where is Robert working now?
3 What does he do there?
4 What job qualification did he get at college?
5 Where did he do his on-the-job training?
6 What is he able to do on the computer?
7 What other skills does he have?
8 What are his free-time interests and hobbies?

E Write a Europass CV for your job. Use the example on p. 154–155 and the texts in Situation 4.3 to help you.

F Go to http://europass.cedefop.europa.eu and create a Language Passport for yourself. Follow the instructions on the screen.

DID YOU KNOW?

Employers don't just look at an employee's CV. They also look for information about you on the internet. Make a list of all the websites where an employer could find information about you. Is the information about you on the internet the same as the information you would write in a CV? Is there anything about you on the internet you would NOT want an employer to see? If so, try to get it removed.

SCENE 3   **Interviewing for a job**

2/8

A   Listen to part 1 of the job interview and say whether the following statements are true or false. Correct the false statements.

1   Dr Joan Calford is the owner of Home Help Manchester.
2   Peter is applying for the job of Assistant Carer to the Eldery.
3   Peter is 25 years old.
4   Peter looked after his sick grandfather.
5   Peter has a driving licence but no car.

B   Listen again and answer the following questions.

1   What qualification does Peter have?
2   When he was a student, what job did Peter have?
3   Why doesn't Peter need his own car?

C   Work in pairs. Here is a list of typical interview questions. Which questions has Dr Calford already asked Peter?

1   Would you please tell me a little bit about yourself?
2   Is this your first job?
3   What qualifications do you have?
4   What other experience do you have?
5   Where do you want to be in five years?
6   Why do you want to be a … ?
7   Do you have a driving licence?
8   What are your greatest strengths and weaknesses?
9   Do you have any questions for me?

D   Listen to the end of the interview again. What does Peter say his strengths and weaknesses are?

2/9

E   Listen to part 2. In pairs, make notes of the questions that Peter asks Dr Calford. What other questions would you ask?

F   From the list of questions in exercise C, decide which questions are relevant to your job, or future job, and prepare your own answers.

G   Tell your partner what job you will apply for in the future and role-play the interview. Partner A, turn to File 23 on p. 144. Partner B, turn to FIle 26 on p. 145.

Your first day at work

Set-up

A   Talk with a partner about your first day at work or at vocational school. What did you do? How did you feel?

 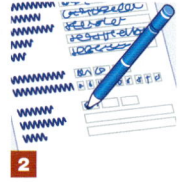  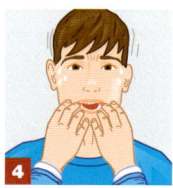 

arrived on time / late	filled out forms	took notes	felt nervous	felt confident

B   Read the tips in the text, then match the headings a–h on p. 99 to the most suitable paragraphs.

Tips for surviving your first day at work
by Amanda Evans

Here are a few tips for making your first day the best it can be.

1   Start the day right
Get a good night's sleep, get up early and eat a good breakfast. That's the best way to kick-start your day.

2
Get there on time. There's nothing worse than arriving late on your first day. It makes a bad impression.

To get there on time, make sure you know how to get to work – which train should you catch and which way do you walk from there?

 Make sure you know where to go. Maybe you have to go to a different location than where your interview was. Training often takes place at a different location.

 Be ready to spend a lot of time filling out paperwork. Don't expect to do much real work on your first day.

 You'll need to bring your tax and bank account details so that you can get paid for all the hard work you do.

 Don't make too many jokes on the first day or act very silly. This also makes a bad impression.

8 It's a good idea to write everything down when people give you instructions. This makes a good impression.

bank account	Bankkonto
impression	Eindruck
instructions	Anweisungen
silly	albern
tax	Steuer

a **Be in the right place**
b **Bring important information**
c ~~**Start the day right**~~
d **Take notes**
e **Be serious**
f **It may be a bit boring**
g **Plan your way to work**
h **Don't be late**

2/10

C Watch or listen to the four speakers talk about their first days at work. What advice from the text didn't they follow?

1 – didn't get a good night's sleep, …

D Did you make any mistakes on your first day of work/school? What would you do differently? Tell your partner.

E Write four tips for international students working at your job or going to your school. Use the following phrases from the text.

1   Make sure …
2   Be ready to …
3   You'll need (to) …
4   It's a good idea to …

SCENARIO B

SCENE 1

Writing your timetable for your first morning

KMK

A Sie sind ein neuer Praktikant bei Besterman AG. Sie haben den unten stehenden Brief von Besterman erhalten.

Lesen Sie den Brief durch. Entscheiden Sie, ob nachfolgende Aussagen richtig oder falsch sind und begründen Sie dies auf Deutsch. Beantworten Sie dann die Verständnisfragen in kurzen Stichworten auf Deutsch.

Dear [your name]

Welcome to Besterman (Italia)! You will be part of a group of trainees who will join us from different parts of the Besterman International Group on Monday, 1st October. Here in Rome, you will learn about Besterman's international operations. Because the trainee group is large, we would like to introduce you to the company in three groups – A, B and C. On the first morning, your programme will look like this:

	9.00	10.30	12.00
Training programme introduction – at the Training Centre	A	B	C
Factory tour – with Production	C	A	B
Paperwork & interview – with Human Resources	B	C	A

We want to divide you alphabetically as follows:
Group A: family name beginning with A-G
Group B: family name beginning with H-N
Group C: family name beginning with O-Z

We look forward to seeing you at your first activity at 9.00. Please be on time!

Yours sincerely

Pietro Calvani

Pietro Calvani
Manager, Human Resources

Aussagen
1 Pietro Calvani arbeitet für die italienische Niederlassung von Besterman.
2 Sie sind der einzige Praktikant, der für diese Veranstaltung aus dem Ausland kommt.
3 Alle Praktikanten sollen sich um 9 Uhr im Training-Center treffen.

Fragen
4 Was ist der Grund für Ihre Reise zu Besterman Italia?
5 Warum werden die Praktikanten in Gruppen aufgeteilt?
6 Wo sollen Sie sich um 12 Uhr befinden (entsprechend Ihrem Nachnamen)?
7 In welcher Abteilung arbeitet Pietro Calvani?

B Copy and write out your complete timetable for 1 October.

Time	Activity	Department
9.00	...	...

SCENE 2

Directions around a company

2/11

A Trainee Felipe has arrived at Besterman's visitors' entrance at 8.45, ready to go to his first activity. Look at the company plan, listen to a security officer's directions, and follow his path with your finger. What is his destination?

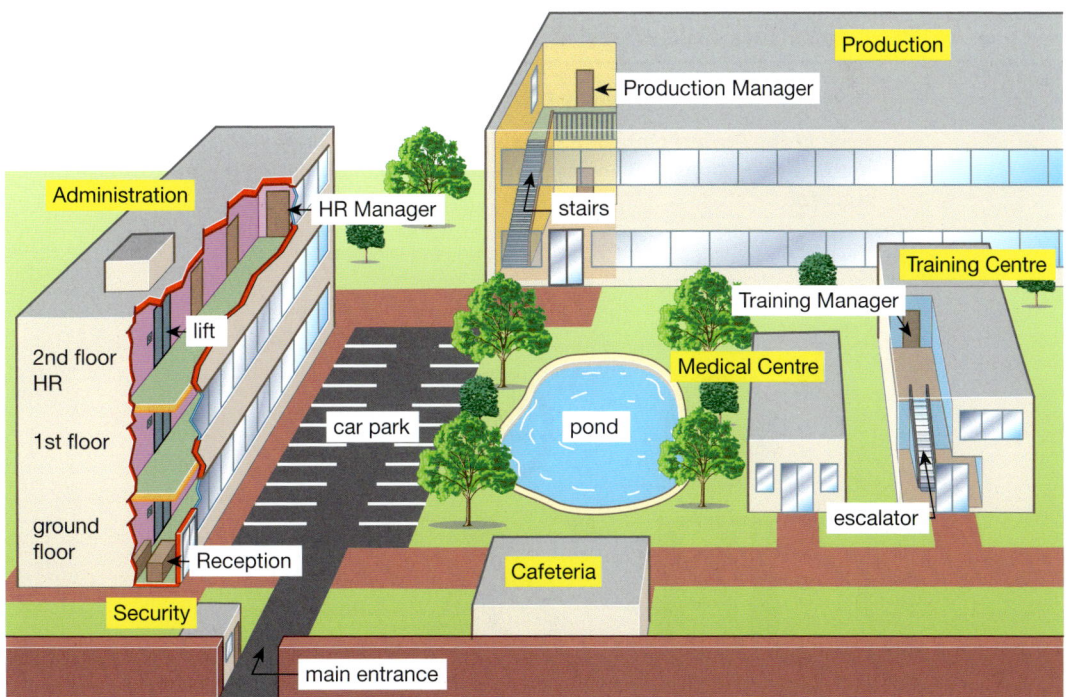

USEFUL LANGUAGE

How do I get to ... ?
Go out of here and turn left/right.
Go straight across / along / round the ...
Go past the ... on your left/right.
Take the escalator/lift/stairs to the first/second floor.
... and it's straight ahead.
You can't miss it!

B It is 10.15. You and two other trainees are having a quick coffee at the cafeteria. You are all between your first and second activities:

Person:	First activity:	Second activity:
Trainee A:	the Training Centre	Production
Trainee B:	HR	the Training Centre
Trainee C:	Production	HR

Work alone and study the route from your first activity to the cafeteria. Then take a minute to describe it silently to yourself.

C Work in groups of three and take the roles of A, B and C. Take turns to ask the way to your next activity. The person who has just come from there gives directions to the department manager's office.

SCENE 3

Presentation on safety signs

Before you can go on the company tour, you must learn about safety signs at work.

A Look at the PowerPoint slide showing safety signs. Work with a partner and match safety signs 1–8 and their meanings a–h. Make notes in your exercise book, e.g. *1c.*

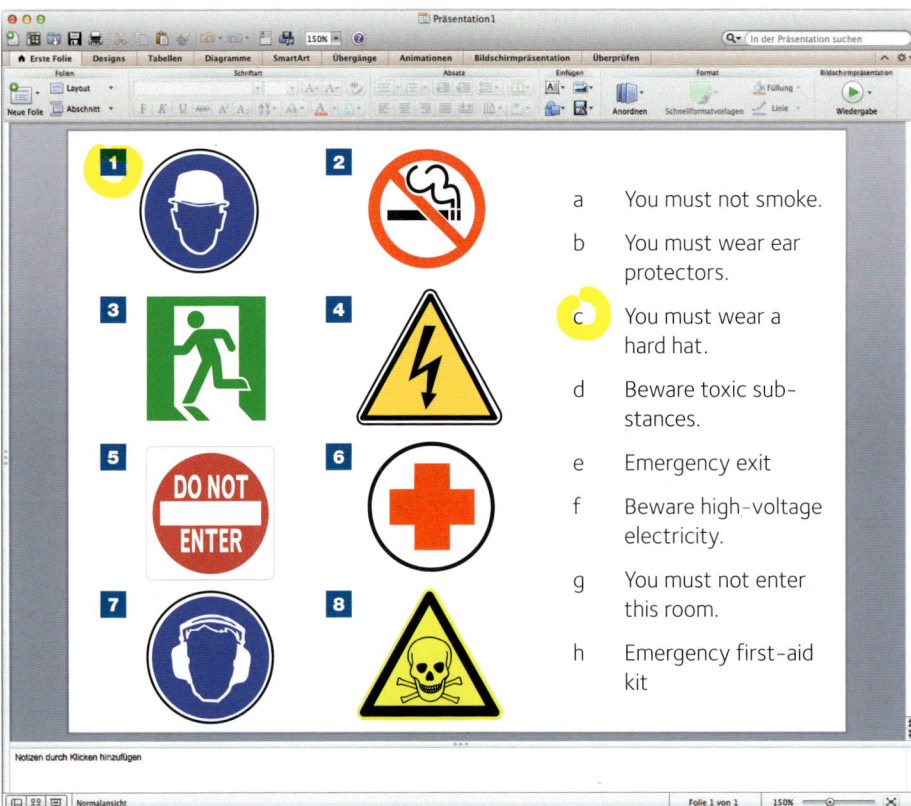

B **Listen to the trainer and trainees. Take over from the trainees as you listen and give your answers from A.**

2/12

Trainer	All right then, let's check your answers. And let's jump around a bit. What about safety sign 7? What does number 7 mean?
Trainee 1	That's: 'You must wear ear protectors.'
Trainer	That's right, and you'll see that sign where there's lots of noise. And how about safety sign 3? What does number 3 mean?
Trainee 2	That means: 'Emergency exit.'
Trainer	Right. So that's really important if there's a fire. And what about safety sign 5?
Trainee (You)	…

C **Look at the PowerPoint slide showing safety sign designs 1–4. Work with a partner and match them to meanings a–d. Make notes in your exercise book, e.g. *1d*.**

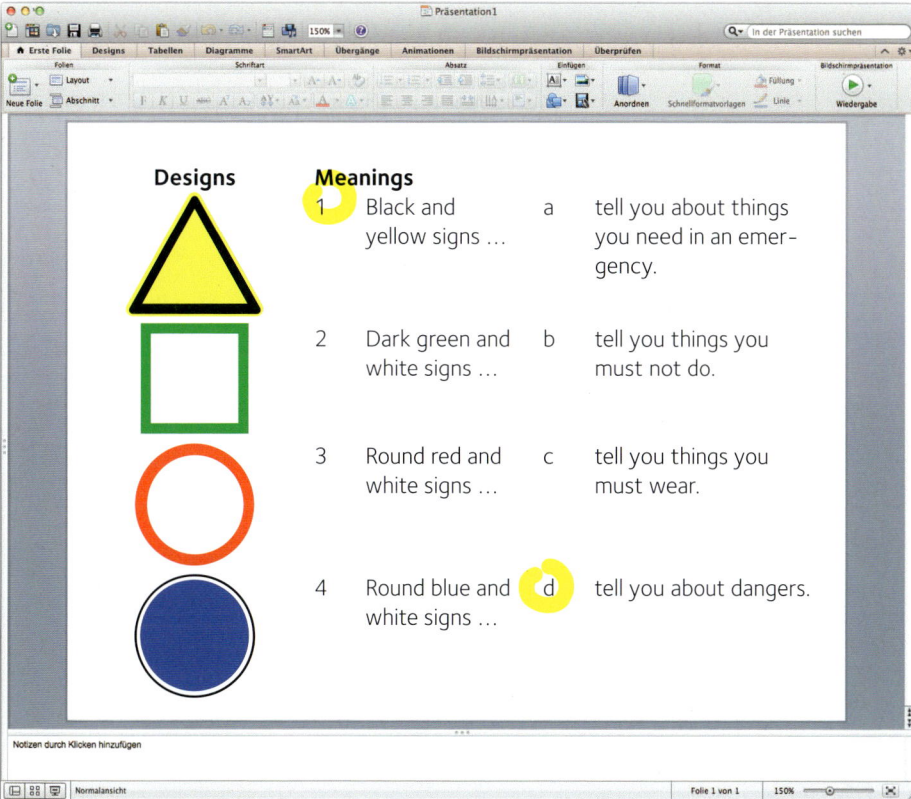

D **Listen and check your answers.**

2/13

E **Work with a partner and play the roles of the trainer and trainee. Start like this.**

Trainer	So what do black and yellow signs tell you?
Trainee	They tell you about …
Trainer	For example?
Trainee	For example, 'Beware toxic …' and 'Beware high-voltage …'.
Trainer	And what do …

SCENE 4

Introduction to your computer

It is after lunch, and the trainees are back in the Training Centre. The IT instructor is showing everyone how to do simple things on the Besterman computer system. These include reading e-mails and communicating formally by e-mail.

A Work with a partner and match the instructions in Step 1 to the pictures. Then do the same for Step 2.

Step 1: Getting into your e-mails

1 First, …

2 Then …

3 Next, …

a … you select the letter icon to access your e-mails.

b … you click on the browser icon to access the internet.

c … you type in your user name and password.

access	aufrufen
select	wählen

Step 2: Dealing with your e-mails

1 First, …

2 Then …

Meet for coffee
Welcome to Besterman
Re: Your first day at work
Fw: Schedule
Car parking spaces

3 Next, …

Welcome to

4 After that, … Welcome to Besterm
Re: Your first day at v

a … you click on REPLY to answer your other e-mails.

b … you click on DELETE to get rid of e-mails that you don't want or no longer need.

c … you click on the e-mails one by one to open and read them.

d … you go to your inbox to find a list of your e-mails.

delete	löschen
get rid of	loswerden
one by one	eins nach dem anderen
reply	beantworten

B Listen to check your work. Then work with a partner and take the parts of the trainer and a trainee. Act out the conversations in Step 1 and Step 2. Use the phrases in A.

2/14

C Work with a partner and match the instructions in Step 3 to the pictures. You have to continue each instruction 1–6 with a phrase a–f and finish with i–vi.

Step 3: Writing e-mails

1 First, …

2 Then …

3 Next, …

SALES REPORT|

4 After that, …

Kind regards |

5 Then …

the report and and we should

6 Finally, …

> briefly — knapp
> recipient — Empfänger

a … you write in the subject line	**i** … to find any mistakes.
b … you click on SEND	**ii** … to say what the e-mail is about.
c … you click on the WRITE button	**iii** … to save everyone time.
d … you go to your e-mail address book	**iv** … to get the e-mail to the recipient.
e … you check your e-mail carefully	**v** … to open a new e-mail window.
f … you write as briefly as possible	**vi** … to select the addressee.

2/15

D Listen to check your work. Then work with a partner and take the parts of the trainer and a trainee. Act out the conversation in Step 3.

E Write out some FAQs (Frequently Asked Questions) about e-mailing. Then write the answers.

Q *How do I correct any spelling mistakes?*

A *First, you mark the text for checking. Next, you click on the spellchecker. Finally, …*

How do I	correct any spelling mistakes?
How can I	draw attention to an important piece of text?
	add a smiley to my e-mail?
	add a file to my e-mail?

> attachment — Anhang
> file — Datei
> mark — markieren

First,	Next,	Finally,
click on 'Attachments'.	select the emoticon icon.	click on a colour.
mark the right place for it.	click on the spellchecker.	click 'Select' to add it.
mark the piece of text.	find the file that you want.	click on your favourite.
mark the text for checking.	go to the highlighter icon.	correct the mistakes the computer finds.

SCENARIO B

SCENE 5 — Writing formal e-mails

The trainer wants to make sure your e-mails make a good impression on customers and other important people. He asks you all to read and improve an e-mail.

A Before you start, turn to p. 158 and quickly read the guidelines for writing formal e-mails.

B Read the e-mail below. It is for a new business contact. Find ten things that are wrong with it, including spelling mistakes. Write it out again with your corrections.

What's wrong with this e-mail?

Hi Mr Kawalski

It was good to meet and talk about our new produt range at the Hannover Messe last Sat!

I was especially intrested to learn that your company is considering an order for 100 cases of Wash-Away. This is VERY good news!!!

If there is any more info that you need, pls contact me at any time.

Best wishes

Boris Shaffer

SCENE 6 — Meeting with an important person

It is later in the afternoon, and the trainees are now back with Human Resources. The HR staff are having short meetings with the trainees one by one.

A Read Part 1 of the conversation when Richard Hueber meets one of the HR staff. Match answers a–g to gaps 1–7. Then listen to check your answers.

2/16

Staff member	Ah, good afternoon, Mr Hueber.
Richard	1 …
Staff member	Please come in and have a seat.
Richard	2 …
Staff member	Well, first of all, welcome to Besterman (Italia).
Richard	3 …
Staff member	How was your journey to Italy?
Richard	4 …
Staff member	When did you get here?
Richard	5 …
Staff member	And how are you enjoying your first day here with us?
Richard	6 …
Staff member	Are there any problems that you'd like to talk about?
Richard	7 …

a Thank you very much.
b I arrived yesterday evening.
c Good afternoon, Mrs Pertini.
d Thank you. It's good to be here.
e Everything went well, thank you.
f No, everything's fine at the moment.
g Very much, thank you. It's going very well.

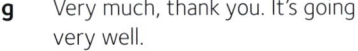

2/17

B   Copy the following table and then listen to the second part of the conversation. Act as Mrs Pertini's assistant and note Richard's answers (in German).

Name	Herkunft	Ausbildungsprogramm	Ausbildungsdauer	Interessen	Ziele
Hueber, Richard					

C   Work with a partner and role-play meeting an important person. Take the parts of an HR Staff Member like Mrs Pertini and of yourself as a Trainee like Richard Hueber.

Before you begin:
- Decide what order you will ask the questions as the Staff Member.
- Prepare answers to give as the Trainee.

Act out first Part 1 and then Part 2 of the interview.

Part 1

Partner A: Trainee
Partner B: HR Staff Member

The Staff Member asks the Trainee the following questions:

> How was your journey to Italy?
> When did you get here?
> Ah, good afternoon, (name).
> Please come in and have a seat.
> Are there any problems that you'd like to talk about?
> Well, first of all, welcome to Besterman (Italia).
> So tell me, what parts of your training do you enjoy most?

Part 2

Partner A: HR Staff Member
Partner B: Trainee

The Staff Member asks the Trainee the following questions:

> And how long is your training?
> When will you finish?
> And how are you enjoying your first day here with us?
> Tell me, where are you from in Germany?
> I see, and what sort of job do you hope to have ten years from now?
> And when did you leave your last school?
> So what training programme are you doing in Germany now?

SCENE 7

2/18

Taking notes

Later in the afternoon, there is a meeting between all the trainees and the HR team.

A   Copy the table below and then listen to HR Manager Mr Calvani and his team. In German, add information that you hear to the table. (You will not hear every sort of information about every member of staff.)

B   Work with a partner. Check your notes together and make sure they are the same. If there are differences, ask to listen again and make corrections.

Name	Berufsbe-zeichnung	Zuständigkeits-bereiche	Raum-nummer	Telefon	Sprech-zeiten	Geplante Unternehmungen mit Datum
Pietro Calvani	Manager, Personal	Personaleinstellungen, Verträge, Training				

A trade fair

hotel check-in | small talk | product descriptions | making contacts | follow-up e-mails

Set-up

A Look at the photo from the Grüne Woche trade fair in Berlin. Tell your partner what you think people are doing there.

What is a trade fair?

In Germany there are over 150 trade fairs every year, and the organisers earn almost 3 billion euros from them. A trade fair happens when people and organisations from the same industry or sector meet in a large exhibition hall. Here, people can find new customers, learn new technology and even make new friends. Grüne Woche is one of Germany's biggest trade fairs. At Grüne Woche, you can find fresh food from all over the world.

At the trade fair, every organisation has a stand, and the trade fair begins with people who build the stands. They work for up to a week before the official opening, and they work long hours, but because a trade fair happens only once a year, it can be a fun and exciting time. Many people who build the stands stay at the same hotels and spend time together in the evenings.

When the stands are ready, people display their products. These people are called the exhibitors. At Grüne Woche, most of the products are food. Because the food is fresh, it has to arrive at the last minute. A trade fair normally opens at 10 a.m. and closes at 6 p.m., and during that time, thousands of people walk through the exhibition hall, talking to the exhibitors and trying out their products. Customers can even buy the products directly at the trade fair. At Grüne Woche, they can taste all the food, and if you go every day, you won't have to buy any of your own food for a week! At the same time as people talk to each other, there are also presentations from companies showing new things in the industry – all in all, a trade fair is a loud event.

The exhibitors also talk to each other, and many exhibitors go to the same trade fair every year, so they make friends as well as business partners.

At the end of the trade fair, the same people who built the stands take the stands away. It happens in one day, and there is often a party for all the exhibitors and builders when the work is finished. There are trade fairs for every industry, from cars to medicine, to sailing, and even theatre and comics.

B Read the text and answer the questions.

1 What can you find at Grüne Woche?
2 How does a trade fair begin?
3 What happens after the stands are ready?
4 As well as talking to people, what also happens at a trade fair?
5 What happens when the trade fair is finished?

SCENARIO C

Checking into a hotel

You work for CarryAll, a manufacturer of high-quality bags and backpacks. Every year, the company sends two employees to the Capsule trade fair in Paris to make contacts and find new business. Capsule is a trade fair for the fashion industry. This year, your boss wants you to go with her.

'Most of the people at the trade fair speak English, and my English is terrible,' she says. 'So you have to do most of the talking.'

2/19

A Listen to the conversation. As you listen, write down phrases you think are useful.

B With a partner, explain in German what the following phrases mean.

1 I have a reservation for two nights.
2 How may I help you?
3 What time is breakfast?
4 Is there a gym?
5 What day are you checking out?
6 We would like to go to the museum. What's the best way to get there?
7 Is there anything more I can help you with?
8 Enjoy your stay with us.

gym	Fitnessstudio
stay (noun)	Aufenthalt
stay (verb)	bleiben / sich aufhalten

C With a partner, play out the following dialogue. Use the phrases you learnt from the recording and from exercise B.

'Bonjour!'

'I'm sorry, we don't speak French. Do you speak English?'

'Yes, of course. How may I help you?'

Nennen Sie Ihren Namen und sagen Sie, dass Sie und Ihre Chefin Reservierungen haben.

'Your room numbers are 2123 and 2127. How many nights are you staying?'

Sagen Sie, dass Sie vier Nächte bleiben werden.

Geben Sie dem Gast die Zimmerschlüssel.

Fragen Sie, um wieviel Uhr man frühstücken kann.

Das Frühstück wird zwischen 8.00 Uhr und 10.00 Uhr serviert.

Fragen Sie, ob das Hotel ein Fitnessstudio hat.

Bejahen Sie die Frage und sagen Sie, dass es auch ein Schwimmbad gibt.

▶

Sagen Sie, dass Sie auf die Capsule Messe in der Rue de Turenne gehen. Fragen Sie, wie Sie am einfachsten dorthin kommen.

Am besten ist es, man nimmt ein Taxi. Sagen Sie, dass Sie dem Gast ein Taxi bestellen können.

Nehmen Sie dankend an.

Wünschen Sie dem Gast einen schönen Aufenthalt.

SCENE 2 Making small talk

2/20

A **Listen to the conversation and answer the questions.**

1 What does Guido's company produce?
2 Where is Pamela's clothing store based?
3 Is it Guido's first time at the trade fair?
4 Where is Guido based?
5 When should Guido visit Copenhagen?
6 Why does Guido like Rome more than Paris?
7 What French food does Guido like?
8 What time do they agree to meet for dinner?

B **Below are seven standard small-talk phrases. In their conversation, Pamela and Guido use five of them. Which five?**

1 I'm pleased to meet you.
2 What do you do?
3 Where are you based?
4 What's the weather like in Rome?
5 I've never been to Copenhagen. What's it like?
6 Do you like French food?
7 What movies do you like?

C **In pairs, pretend you are at the trade fair and make small talk about the places you have been and the food you like. Use the Useful Language box to help you.**

USEFUL LANGUAGE

I'm pleased to meet you.

What are you doing at the trade fair?

What do you do?

Have you ever been to … before?

Yes, once / twice / three times.

No, never.

Do you like Italian/Indian/Mexican/ Greek/German food?

My favourite dish is pizza/burritos/ sausage.

SCENARIO C

Talking to other professionals

You are talking to another exhibitor at the trade fair.

A In pairs, practise the following questions and answers. Some questions only have one answer, but others may have more. Mix up the questions and answers and practise saying them so they sound natural.

Questions

Are your bags made from real leather?
Where are your bags made?
How long does it take to make a bag?
What's your best seller?
Is it true that Hollywood stars buy your bags?

Answers

I don't know. I'll have to find out for you.
Mmm, I think so, but I'm not sure.
Yes, that's right.
No, not quite.
The Moto Black is our best seller.

B Below are some more questions professionals often ask each other. On a piece of paper, write down all six questions. Write possible answers to five of the questions and leave one blank. Give the paper to another person in the class.

1 What company are you with?
2 What does your company do?
3 How long has your company been in business?
4 Where are you based?
5 Who are your customers?
6 Do you have a brochure?

C Role-play meeting someone at a trade fair. Begin with 'Hello, how are you?' and then ask and answer the questions. Use the answers you received in B and one answer from A.

SCENE 4

Describing products

A Match the images to the words.

briefcase • suitcase • backpack • handbag • messenger bag

1

2

3

4

5

2/21

B Listen to the conversation between two people at the trade fair and write down the following information.

1 The name of the bag.
2 What the bag is used for.
3 The number of pockets.
4 The available colours.
5 The price.

C Choose another bag from the images in exercise A and write a description like the one you have just heard. Tell it to a partner.

SCENE 5

Trading business cards and contact details

A At a trade fair, people might say the following phrases to you. Organize the phrases into two categories: people who want to give you their contact details, and people who want you to give them your contact details.

1 Do you have a business card?
2 What are your contact details?
3 Here's a brochure. All of our contact details are there.
4 Can I give you my card?
5 What's your e-mail address?
6 Can you give me one of your order forms?
7 Can I send my details to your smartphone?
8 Do you have a pen and paper? Let me write my details for you.

B Look at File 29 on p. 146. Choose one of the cards – that is your business card. Set up the class like a trade fair and walk from stand to stand, talking to each person. Find out what the person's business does, and get their business card. Try to get as many business cards as you can.

USEFUL LANGUAGE

What's your name?
What do you do?
What products do you make?
Where are you based?

SCENARIO C

Writing a follow-up e-mail

A Are the following statements about English e-mails true or false? Correct the false statements. Check your answers in the e-mailing guidelines on p. 158.

1 A formal e-mail begins with 'Dear…'.
2 An e-mail must always end with 'Best Regards'.
3 You should not use many exclamation marks (!).
4 Writing in ALL CAPS is bad style in formal e-mails.
5 You mustn't use smileys or internet slang in work e-mails.
6 You should not use abbreviations in an informal e-mail.

B Two of the following statements are NOT suitable for opening a formal e-mail. Which two?

1 I hope this e-mail finds you well.
2 It was very nice meeting you at the trade fair last week.
3 What's up?
4 I'm writing to enquire about your new product.
5 I don't feel well today, so this e-mail is short.
6 Thank you for your previous e-mail.

★★
C Your boss has written a formal e-mail to one of the people she met at Capsule. Translate it into English for her. Add a suitable opening from exercise B.

Sehr geehrter Herr Sandhurst,

wir haben uns letzte Woche bei der Capsule Messe unterhalten. Ich arbeite für den deutschen Taschenhersteller CarryAll. Sie sagten, dass Sie Interesse daran hätten, unsere Taschen in Ihren Läden zu verkaufen. Wenn Sie immer noch interessiert sind, würde ich gerne ausführlicher mit Ihnen über diese Angelegenheit reden.

Sie können mich unter dieser Mailadresse direkt kontaktieren, oder Sie können unser Büro unter +49 (0) 42 4756 4634 erreichen.

Ich freue mich auf Ihre Antwort.

Mit freundlichen Grüßen

Johanna Schmidt

Leiterin, Verkauf
CarryAll

★ **D** Here is a formal e-mail from a person you met at the Capsule trade fair. Translate it into German for your boss.

Dear Ms Schmidt

I bought one of your bags at Capsule last week, the 'Hiker'. I am writing to tell you that I am very happy with the bag, and I would like to sell it in my shop in Glasgow. Can we order 20 Hiker bags for this month, and 20 bags for next month? Then, if sales are good, we will order more.

Yours sincerely

Reginald Winterbottom

A trip

customer requests | **rescheduling** | **planning travel** | **choosing hotels**

Set-up

A **Skim the text as quickly as possible and answer the following questions.**

  1 What is the subject of the text?
  2 What kind of text is it?
  a an opinion article
  b a personal story
  c an interview with an expert
  d an interview with a tourist

B **Sie arbeiten in einer Firma, in der immer mehr Geschäftsreisen geplant sind.** **KMK**
Viele von Ihren Kollegen haben aber noch nie eine Geschäftsreise gemacht.
Ihr Chef Herr Köpper hat Sie gebeten, den Text ‚It's not all fun in the sun' zu lesen
und dessen Inhalt stichpunktartig in einem Infoblatt namens ‚Wissenswertes über
Geschäftsreisen' an die Belegschaft weiterzugeben, damit sie wissen, was auf sie
zukommt, wenn sie reisen bzw. wenn sie eine Reise planen.

It's not all fun in the sun

By Will McNeice

With the internet and video conferencing tools like Skype, IBM Sametime and OoVoo, it is no longer necessary to travel to see a person's face. There is even holographic video chat, so the person you're talking to appears to be in the same room! You would think that because of this, business trips would become less popular, but you would be wrong. In the United States alone, with a population of 350 million people, there are over 400 million business trips every year, which is more than one business trip per person per year. To find out more about business trips, I talked to Jürgen Schwarz, CEO of IntraPlanet Travel.

Will McNeice: Why do people go on business trips?
Jürgen Schwarz: Business trips are important for big deals because making a deal is not just about talking, but about trust, and trust comes from body language. You can't read body language on a computer screen.

appear	scheinen
CEO	Geschäftsführer
population	Bevölkerung

Article continues on next page →

compare	vergleichen
fancy	extravagant
flight	Flug
local	einheimisch
look forward to s. th.	sich auf etwas freuen
otherwise	ansonsten
research	Recherche

WM: Who organises business trips and how do they do it?

JS: The assistants usually organise the trips for their bosses and colleagues. First, the assistant finds out where the traveller needs to go and when. Then it's time to do research. They have to compare a lot of different flights and train schedules, and also hotels, and they have to stay within the budget.

WM: Do the employees have to pay for anything on the trip?

JS: Not normally. The company pays for everything: for the hotel, for the flights, for taxis and for food and drink. If the employees decide to go to the cinema or eat in a very fancy restaurant, they have to pay for it, but otherwise the company will pay.

WM: How do employees feel about business trips?

JS: It's different from one employee to the next. If an employee takes one trip a year, he or she enjoys it and looks forward to it. If that employee takes one trip a week, it can be stressful, especially if that person has a family. At Intra-Planet Travel, some of us have to travel a lot and, I can tell you, it's not all fun in the sun.

WM: Do employees need to speak English on business trips?

JS: Most of the time, yes. If an employee speaks a local language, that's great. But if not, almost every hotel around the world uses English as the international language. Airports use English, and most international businesses use English too. When we send employees on business trips, at least one of them must speak English.

SCENE 1

Dealing with customer requests

SonnenPower sends out teams from Stuttgart across Europe to install its solar power systems. Erica Hoffman coordinates the work of these teams, and she often has to find quick answers to sudden problems. The latest problem comes from Etoile Construction in the south of France, which is building a supermarket in a new shopping centre near Marseilles.

2/22

A   Listen to the phone conversation and answer the questions.

1   Who is calling?
2   Where is he calling from?
3   What does he want?
4   What does Erica promise to do?

B   Listen again and note the details that Erica needs.

Rescheduling

After Pierre Bertrand's call, Erica e-mailed Production and she soon got a reply. She also got a surprise e-mail from one of the installation teams, now on a job in the UK.

A Read the reply from Herr Taubmann in Production and the e-mail from team leader Paul Bremen. Then answer the questions.

1 From the first e-mail, what can she say to Pierre Bertrand?

2 From the second e-mail, what else can she say to him?

Neue E-Mail

An: Hoffman, Assistentin Bereich Vertrieb

Betreff: Vorzeitige Auslieferung der Bestellung Nummer FR26781

Von: Taubmann   **Signatur:** Ohne

Hallo Frau Hoffman,

danke für Ihre Anfrage. Zum Glück haben wir die Solarkollektoren für Etoile schon fertig. Es ist auch ein Lastwagen verfügbar, um die Baustelle am Montag, dem 15., um 8 Uhr zu beliefern. Wenn Sie das möchten, bestätigen Sie bitte die vorzeitige Auslieferung bis zum Ende des Tages.

Mit freundlichen Grüßen
B. Taubmann, Manager Produktion

Neue E-Mail

An: Hoffman, Assistentin Bereich Vertrieb

Betreff: Frühzeitige Fertigstellung in Oxford, England

Von: Bremen   **Signatur:** Ohne

Hallo Frau Hoffman,

es freut mich, Ihnen mitzuteilen, dass wir die Installation an der Unitech-Fabrikanlage drei Tage früher abschließen werden. Wir müssen an diesem Freitag eine letzte Kontrolle machen, dann sind wir fertig.

Sollen wir direkt nach Stuttgart zurückkommen oder haben Sie andere Pläne? Bitte lassen Sie mich das so bald wie möglich wissen. Werden Sie unsere Flüge umbuchen oder soll ich das machen?

Alles Gute
Paul Bremen, Leiter Blaues Team

B Work with a partner. Act out the next telephone conversation between Erica and Pierre Bertrand. Use File 24 on p. 144 and File 27 on p. 145.

C Work with a partner. Act out the next telephone conversation between Erica and Pierre Bertrand. Use the following structure for your dialogue.

Pierre/Perrine Bertrand (from Etoile)

Eric/Erica Hoffman (from SonnenPower)

Gehen Sie ans Telefon und begrüßen Sie den Anrufer.

Sagen Sie, wer Sie sind.

Danken Sie dem Anrufer für den Rückruf und wiederholen Sie, dass Sie die Solarkollektoren (*panels*) nächste Woche wirklich brauchen.

Sagen Sie, dass Sie eine gute Nachricht haben.

Drücken Sie Ihre Überraschung und gleichzeitige Freude aus. Bitten Sie darum, mehr zu erfahren.

Schildern Sie die Situation in Bezug auf die Kollektoren: Versand ist bis 8 Uhr am Montag, dem 15., möglich.

Sagen Sie, dass das eine sehr gute Nachricht ist. Aber was ist mit der Installation der Kollektoren? Die Bereitstellung der Kollektoren allein reicht nicht.

Erklären Sie, dass ein Team frühzeitig einen Auftrag in England beendet hat und dass es zur Baustelle von Etoile fahren kann.

Sagen Sie, dass Sie wirklich sehr zufrieden sind. Danken Sie Frau/Herrn Hoffman herzlich.

Sagen Sie, dass SonnenPower sich immer freut, wenn sie ihren Kunden helfen können.

Bedanken Sie sich noch einmal und verabschieden Sie sich.

Sagen Sie, dass Sie das gerne gemacht haben und verabschieden Sie sich.

D Play the dialogue again. Try to talk faster than last time.

SCENE 3 | Getting travel information

Erica Hoffman has asked Blue Team to go straight from Oxford to Marseilles on Saturday, ready to start the Etoile Construction job on Monday. Blue Team Leader Paul Bremen makes travel plans with Fast Track Travel in Oxford. He is talking to them now.

2/23

A Copy the notes. Then listen to Paul's conversation with the travel agent and complete his notes.

Possible flights

Time	Cost (single)	Flight No.
1 ...	£ ...	...
2 ...	£ ...	...
3 ...	£ ...	...

2/24

B Copy the notes. Then listen to the conversation between the travel agent and Paul's assistant, Turgut Demirel, and complete his notes.

Travel to the airport

By:	Travel time:	Cost:	Number of changes:
Bus	...	£ ...	...
Train	...	£ ...	...
Taxi	...	£ ...	...

SCENE 4 | Planning travel

A Work with a partner. Take the parts of Paul and Turgut and share your information. Decide the following.

1 which flight to take
2 how the team will travel to the airport

(Think about doing things as easily and as comfortably as possible. After a hard week's work, Turgut does not want to get up too early on Saturday morning. And Paul does not want to arrive too late. They should also try to keep costs down as much as possible. See File 25 on p. 144 and File 28 on p. 145 for summaries of the information that Paul and Turgut have now got.)

B Take Paul's part and write his e-mail to Erica. Explain how Blue Team will travel to Marseilles, with full details.

SCENE 5

Choosing a hotel

Erica now has to find five single hotel rooms in France for Blue Team. She is worried because it is very late to do this.

A Read Erica's criteria and about the hotels in the area.

Kriterien für die Hotelwahl
- Die fünf Personen vom Blue Team im Idealfall im selben Hotel unterbringen; wenn das nicht möglich: die Gruppe auf keinen Fall auf mehr als zwei Hotels verteilen.
- Das Hotel/Die Hotels sollte/n so nah wie möglich an der Baustelle von Etoile liegen (im Stadtzentrum von Gardanne).
- Die Unterkunft soll komfortabel, aber trotzdem günstig sein.
- Nicht vergessen: einen hotelnahen, sicheren Parkplatz einplanen (nicht an einer Hauptverkehrsstraße). Und: Das Team benötigt nach Ankunft direkt am Flughafen einen Leihwagen für sieben Tage!

Availability	
Room type:	Single
Arriving:	14 March
Departing:	20 March
Number of available beds: 3	

Hotel Chemin du Dort ✴✴

We are a small, friendly, family-run hotel located just outside the pretty country town of Gardanne. We look out over open country but we are just a kilometre from the centre of town.

All our rooms are en suite, with showers, and they offer free wi-fi.

We serve breakfast daily from 6.30 to 9.30, and we can also offer packed lunches.

Free parking for a small number of cars. Further nearby on-road parking is possible.

Prices start from € 70 for a single.

Map labels: E80, Aix-en-Provence, Hotel Chemin du Dort, D7, A8, Gardanne, A51, D8, A52, D7, Marseille, A50, 5 km

availability	Verfügbarkeit
en suite	mit Bad/Dusche und WC
facilities	Ausstattung
family-run	familiär geführt
secure	sicher
single	Einzelzimmer

Availability	
Room type:	Single
Arriving:	14 March
Departing:	20 March
Number of available beds: 3	

Logis Bel Air ✳✳✳

We are just two kilometres off the fast A 51 from Marseille (15 km) to Aix-en-Provence (11 km). So we offer a quiet place in the country after a busy day in the big city, complete with beautiful flower gardens. We are also only a short way (3 km) from the centre of the attractive town of Gardanne, with its shops and daily market.

Our rooms, all en suite and all with flat-screen TVs, also offer free wi-fi.

Our prices include breakfast, and guests are also welcome at our Bel Air Brasserie for light meals at other times of the day.

Prices are from € 85 for a single to € 145 for a large family room.

Large, secure car park available.

Availability	
Room type:	Single
Arriving:	14 March
Departing:	20 March
Number of available beds: 2	

Pont de L'Arc ✳✳✳✳

This fine hotel stands on a large piece of land just two kilometres south of the centre of Aix-en-Provence and six kilometres from the attractive old town of Gardanne. Marseille is just over 20 kilometres away. With its outdoor swimming pool and attractive gardens, this is the perfect centre for a family holiday in the heart of Provence.

Our rooms are all en suite (with shower and bath), and they offer flat-screen TVs, free wi-fi and facilities for making tea and coffee.

Our friendly, multi-lingual staff are ready to help you in any way they can in nearly every European language.

Prices are from € 95 a night for a single to € 160 for a large family room.

Prices include use of car park and swimming pool.

B   Compare each hotel with Erica's criteria. Decide where to put the members of the Blue Team and explain why.

C   Write an e-mail to Paul Bremen to explain what you have booked for him and his team and why.

A company party

planning | setting dates | choosing locations | planning menus

Set-up

A **Tell your partner about the last party you went to.**

B **Read the text and answer the questions.**

1 Why do people have parties?
2 What happens at a surprise party?
3 What types of work-related parties does the article talk about?
4 Which kind of party is not always a happy event?
5 What must you not do at a work-related party? Why?

Having a party at work

What's the difference between a business meeting and a party? Both happen when a group of people meet. You can eat and drink at both. Both can be fun and both can be boring. So how is a business meeting different from a party?

The difference is the reason for meeting. People have a business meeting to solve a problem or to plan a project, and people have a party to celebrate something. When you have a party for a person, it can be a surprise party, or a normal party. If it's a surprise, people usually turn off the lights and hide behind furniture and wait for the person to arrive. When he or she enters the room, everybody jumps out and shouts, 'Surprise!' Some people like surprises; some don't.

Work-related parties are more common than people think, and co-workers can always find a reason to have fun both inside and outside of the office. The most common party is the birthday party. In some companies the birthday party involves a short song and a cake, while in other companies it can be a whole evening at a restaurant or a bar.

The next most popular party is the Christmas party. Usually in the first or second week of December, the Christmas party is a big event for most companies. The company normally pays for the food and there is often lots of alcohol. Christmas parties can sometimes be wild!

When a department reaches its targets or the company wins a major contract, people want to celebrate. These parties are normally smaller.

The last important type of work-related party is the goodbye party. The goodbye party happens when an employee retires or leaves the company to work somewhere else. Everybody at the company gives some money for a present, and a goodbye party can sometimes be a sad event.

If you go to a work-related party, you must remember that your boss is still your boss, and you must be respectful. Don't drink too much alcohol and don't say anything bad to your boss or to other employees. If you do, you might find yourself unemployed the next day!

celebrate	feiern
contract	Vertrag
surprise	Überraschung
target	Ziel

SCENE 1 | **Planning**

The trainees' time at Besterman (Italia) has nearly finished, and they are planning a goodbye party. The first thing to decide is the date of the party. You are the party committee's secretary, and you have to take notes on all decisions that are made.

2/25

A   Listen to the discussion and note the only possible date for the party.

Monday	Tuesday	Wednesday	Thursday	Friday	Saturday	Sunday
22	23	24	25	26	27	28

B   Listen again and answer the questions.

1   What is important about Friday 26th?
2   Can the party be on Monday, Tuesday or Wednesday? Explain.
3   Can the party be on the 26th? Explain.
4   How many people can they expect to come to the party?
5   What do they want to do about music?
6   What do they want to do about food?

C   Write five tweets to post on your social networking pages, so everyone at Besterman finds out about the party. You want to hype the party as much as possible. Each tweet can be a maximum of 140 characters. Write about the following.

- How excited you are about the party, how much you are looking forward to it, etc.
- The date of the party
- How many people you expect to come
- What the music and food will be like
- The location has not been chosen yet – suggestions are welcome!

Silke Meyer
Our goodbye party at Besterman is going to be awesome! #byebyebesterman
Like   Comment

SCENARIO E

SCENE 2 | ## Choosing locations

Next, the committee must find the best place for the party, and they agree on the following list of criteria.

A place for our party – important criteria:
- Must be available on the right night – until about midnight
- Must be big enough
- Must be cheap – or (better) free!
- Must be easy to get to – either at Besterman or somewhere in town but very near (Remember: we will have to carry food there, and other things too.)
- Must have a kitchen to prepare food
- Must have tables and chairs for people to sit down and eat, plus plates, etc.
- Must have a sound system for music

The committee also agree that different people will check different possible places. They will then write short reports for the next committee meeting to discuss.

A First, copy and complete the table. Then check the three reports against the criteria above. Write notes in the table with points for and against each place.

	Am 25. bis 0 Uhr ok?	Größe ok?	Kosten?	Einfach zu erreichen?	Küche vorhanden?	Tische, Geschirr etc.?	Musikanlage?
Firmenkantine	✔	✔	müssten Kantinenessen kaufen				
Stadthalle							

The company cafeteria
Besterman's cafeteria is open 24 hours a day every day for people in Production, and we can also use it any night. The Manager, Paula Silvestrini, says we can use a part of it for our party. There's a sound system here, and so we can have music too – if it isn't too loud. And it won't cost us anything, she says. But we can't prepare our own food here: we have to have the food they make – and we have to pay for it in the usual way.

The town's community hall
- Can be available on the night that we want
- Easily big enough for 100 people
- The Manager, Nina Carluccio, says we can have it for €150, so that's just €5 for each of us trainees. Not too bad!
- It's about 2 kilometres across town.
- There's a kitchen, but we have to bring our own plates, glasses, etc.
- Has tables and chairs
- There's a sound system, but we can't use it after 10.00 because of the neighbours. (We also have to finish by 11.00.)

The Besterman staff club meeting room
It isn't very big, but it's big enough. And it's available on the right night.

Manager Franco Moro says we can prepare food in the kitchen there. He just asks for some money for electricity and for any plates or glasses that we break – perhaps €100, he says.

There's a sound system, so music isn't a problem, and there are enough chairs, but there are only four tables. We can use the place until 12.00 at night, but we must leave the kitchen and the hall clean and tidy, ready for others to use the next day.

B   **Work with 2–3 partners and take the parts of committee members. Discuss points for and against the three possible party locations: first the cafeteria, then the community hall, and finally the staff club meeting room. Choose the best place. Agree on answers to problems.**

USEFUL LANGUAGE

I feel the [place]	is / isn't	the	right / best	one.	First of all, it's … / For one thing, it's …	Secondly, it's … / For another, it's …
I feel the [place]	is / isn't	the	right / best	choice, because …		
If we choose the [place],		we'll / we won't	be able to … / have to … / need to …			

I think you're right (about that).
You've got a point, but I also think ...
I'm not sure about that. I feel/think ...

Planning a menu

A party isn't very good without food. The committee agrees that each trainee will bring a dish. It can be from their own country or any other. They will prepare their dishes – with labels – and put them on the buffet table, ready for everyone to try.

A   Read the labels 1-5 and match them to the dishes a-e.

 Paella
A main course from Spain, made with rice, chicken, vegetables and seafood

 **Torrijas**
A warm dessert from Mexico, made with bread and honey

3 **Salad niçoise**
A salad from France, made with tuna and other fish and various vegetables

4 **Scotch broth**
A soup from Scotland, made with lamb and vegetables

5 **Florida fruit cocktail**
A cold starter from the USA, made with mixed fruit

a   b   c   d   e

B   Work in a group and agree on a menu with a dish from each person. (Try to choose things that you really can make.)

C   Write out the menu.

D   Work with a new partner, who takes the part of someone from another country and wants you to explain each item on your menu.

Putting plans in writing

★★ **A**   Write a letter in English to the Manager of the place you want to use for the party. Ask politely for the use of the place, and give the following information.

- The date and times that you need it
- The probable number of guests
- The things that you will need for the party
- The way that people will use the kitchen
- The price that you will pay (if you have to pay)
- When the party will finish and how you will leave the place

★ **B**   **Write an e-mail invitation to the party. It should do the following.**

- Give the date, time and place
- Say who is giving the party
- Show the purpose of the party
- Highlight the international theme of the party

1 **When might you use the following expressions? Sort them under the headings a) meeting someone you don't know, b) meeting someone again.**

1 Are you John Doe?
2 Good afternoon. I'm Linda Wilson. Welcome to …
3 Good morning, Mary. How are you today?
4 Hello, Martin. How was your flight?
5 It's nice to meet you.
6 It's nice to see you again.
7 Klaus! How are things?
8 Welcome to London. I'm Jane Roe.

2 **Read the text and say where these headings should go: paragraph A, B, C or D.**

1 **Be polite**
2 **Be prepared**
3 **Communication or correct English?**
4 **Pay attention to your visitor**

How to welcome a visitor

Wherever you work and whatever you do, you may have to welcome a visitor to your company one day. Here are some tips for getting it right.

A
Before the visitor arrives
– make sure you know his/her name and how to pronounce it properly.
– find out where the visitor is from.
– if you haven't been told already, ask the purpose of the visit and who he/she is visiting.

B
When the visitor arrives
– introduce yourself clearly using your first name and your surname.
– say 'Nice to meet you.' or 'Pleased to meet you.'
– shake hands.
– ask a question, for example, 'Did you have a good trip?'
– make the visitor feel comfortable. Ask, 'Can I take your coat?' or 'Would you like a cup of coffee?'

C
Remember to listen carefully to what the visitor says.

D
Last but not least, remember that you don't have to speak perfect English. Just be business-like but friendly. That's the most important thing.

1 Some business people made the following list of activities that they find difficult when they speak English on the telephone. Which points do you think are the most difficult and least difficult? Give reasons for your answers.

a answering a call
b checking the computer while the caller is talking
c getting dates and numbers right
d ending a call politely
e taking a message
f transferring a call
g understanding e-mail addresses
h understanding people's names
i when a bad line makes communication difficult

Can we speak English?

2 Match the points above to the tips on the poster. There is one more tip than you need.

Ten tips for telephoning

1 Always have paper and a pen beside the phone to note things down. Don't make the caller wait if he/she wants you to pass on information.

2 Ask the caller to 'please hold the line'. Then say, 'I'll put you through now.' If the other person doesn't pick up, tell the caller. Offer to try another number or to take a message.

3 Ask the caller to repeat something you haven't understood. If there's a problem with the phone, say, 'Sorry, you're breaking up.'

4 Ask the caller to spell their name if it's difficult.

5 Repeat the information in a different form. If the caller says a date as, 'twenty-one – six – seventy-two' you can say, 'So that's the twenty-first of June, nineteen-seventy-two.' Repeat each digit separately, except for double digits, e.g. 012334567899 = 'oh one two double-three four five six seven eight double-nine.'

6 Say every bit of a web address again carefully, repeating things like 'dot' or 'at'.

7 Say your name and the name of the company. Say, 'How can I help you?'

8 Smile. This is the only body language signal you can use on the phone. Use it to create a positive, helpful atmosphere right from the start.

9 Tell the caller what you're doing. Say, 'Just a moment, please. Let me check that.'

10 Thank the caller using his/her name. Say, 'It was nice talking to you.'

1 Which of these things can you talk about when you make small talk at work? What should you <u>not</u> talk about? Make two lists.

> books • films • food • hobbies • holidays • money • music • politics • problems at home • religion • sport • weather

2 All five of these statements are incorrect. Correct them using information from the text.

1 Annie thinks small talk is good for business.
2 Bill the Blogger has never made small talk in a business situation.
3 Clever Cathy has no idea how to make small talk.
4 Dave the Dude says you can talk about anything when you make small talk.
5 Educated Ellen says it's important to talk good English when you make small talk.

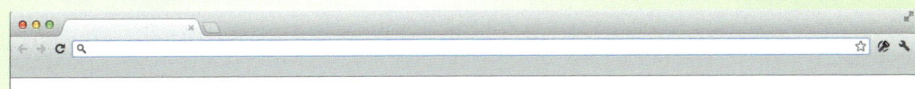

Subject: How important is small talk?

Annie
Small talk is polite conversation about ordinary or unimportant subjects. It's just a way to make friendly conversation and not much use in business.

Bill the Blogger
@Annie – I don't agree. I think small talk is important in business. I had an interview last week. At the start, the employer said, 'Did you find us all right?' and I said, 'Yes, thank you. I checked the directions on your website.' It was only a short question and answer, but this little bit of small talk helped me to relax before the interview started.

Clever Cathy
Bill the Blogger is right. Small talk always helps when you meet new business partners. It makes people feel comfortable before meetings and helps to break the ice. Ask a new person some questions, then pay attention to the answers to keep the conversation going.

Dave the Dude
@Clever Cathy – I'd like to add a couple of points. Don't ask questions that only need a yes/no answer. 'Where are you going on holiday this year?' is better than 'Are you going on holiday this year?' And think carefully about the topics you choose. Talk about sport, films or music. Don't talk about sex, politics, religion, money or private problems.

Educated Ellen
Don't be afraid to make small talk. Even if your English isn't very good, when someone starts up a conversation with you, relax and be natural. You'll really enjoy making small talk.

break the ice	das Eis brechen
ordinary	alltäglich
pay attention	genau zuhören
polite	höflich
topic	Thema

1 Sometimes you have to wear special clothes at work. Find the following items of clothing in the pictures: a hard hat, a lab coat, overalls, an apron, a uniform.

scientist

waitress

builder

mechanic

shop keeper

2 Read the text and find the correct places (Q1–Q4) for the following questions a–d.

a How can I make a good impression at an interview?
b How will I know what to wear?
c What is company culture?
d What should I look for when I check out the company?

Job basics – fitting in at work

You've found an interesting job advertisement and you're thinking of applying for the position. But, stop! Before you go any further, check out the company online to find out if you'd fit in.

Read our **FAQs** on this subject.

Q1: …

A: Try to find anything which tells you about company culture.

Q2: …

A: Company culture is made up of the values of the organization and the ways of behaviour that are the normal way of doing things in the organization. For example, are employees allowed to use the computer for personal e-mails? How should you talk to your colleagues? Who can you address with their first name? All these things, and many more, make up the 'culture' of a company.

Q3: …

A: Some organizations have a dress code which usually says what not to wear. For example, in banks and insurance companies, the employees are often asked not to wear jeans. Some companies give their employees special clothes. This can be a uniform so that everyone looks the same, or it can be protective clothing which you have to wear for health or safety reasons.

Q4: …

A: Wear something neutral. Don't wear too much jewellery and be careful with your hair and make-up. Whatever the job, the most important thing is to look clean and neat. Check the company website for photos of younger employees and try to wear the same sort of clothes when you go for the interview.

behaviour	Benehmen
FAQ (Frequently Asked Question)	häufig gestellte Frage
fit in	sich einfügen
impression	Eindruck
insurance	Versicherung
make up	ausmachen
protective clothing	Schutzkleidung
value	Wert

1 Before you read the text, scan it and find the following facts as quickly as possible.

a a reason why Europeans are so mobile
b the number of native speakers of English in the world
c the number of people in the European Union who are living in a foreign country

foreign	fremd
foreigner	Ausländer
limited	begrenzt
native speaker	Muttersprachler
supplier	Lieferant

THE JOB COACH BLOG

FRANCOIS DUCHAMPS

About   E-mail

English: why Europeans need it

We Europeans are extremely mobile. Many of us move to other countries within Europe and further away. Many more leave their countries for short periods to do internships and jobs, to go on business trips, and to take holidays. This is now easier than ever to do, especially within the EU. Here, you don't need a special visa and you don't need to say goodbye to your homeland forever. You can go back there as often as you wish. You can leave as often as you need to for your job. But there is one thing that everyone needs for international travel which takes a long time to get: competence in English.

Why English? Just look at the statistics. English is the language that most people in Europe (and probably the whole world) understand. There are 'only' about 350 million native speakers of English in the world, but the number of people who speak it as a foreign language is much higher. People all over the world do half of all business deals and write 70 percent of all mail in English.

Even if you never leave your country, the English speakers come to you. There are more than 21 million people living as foreigners in the EU. If you live in Germany, France or the UK, you are getting more foreign neighbours every year, and the language that most of them can speak is English. I speak English with many of my customers. I wouldn't have as many customers if I spoke only my native language. It's the same for you if you work in a shop, a restaurant, an office, in health care or as a technician. If you can speak English, you get more customers, and employers love you for it. With English, you are also able to communicate with your employer's foreign suppliers, its mother and sister companies and all other foreign partners. Without English, a European's chances for success are really limited.

2 Which of the following is *not* given as a reason why English is important?

a Europeans often move from country to country.
b English is the language which allows you to communicate with the most people in Europe.
c If you speak English, you have more potential customers.
d If you understand English, you can find out about new developments in your profession which come from other countries.

3 Work in a group and make a list of situations when you would use English in your job and in your free time.

Schriftliche Prüfung

1
Rezeption: Hörverstehen

2/26

Sie machen ein Praktikum bei einer Firma in England. Ein Kollege bittet Sie, seinen Anrufbeantworter abzuhören und den Inhalt des Anrufs für ihn zu notieren.

Lesen Sie sich das Formular durch. Übertragen Sie die Vorlage auf ein Blatt Papier und füllen Sie sie auf Deutsch aus. Sie hören die Nachricht zwei Mal. Während des Hörens können Sie sich Notizen machen.

Green Inc.

1 Name des Anrufers: …
2 Name und Sitz der Firma des Anrufers: …
3 Telefonnummer des Anrufers: …
4 Welches Anliegen hat der Anrufer? …
5 Warum ist eine schnelle Lösung erforderlich? …

6 Welchen Vorschlag macht der Anrufer? …
7 An wen soll das Problem ggf. weitergeleitet werden? …
8 Wann kann der Anrufer zurückgerufen werden? …

TELEFONNOTIZ

2
Rezeption: Leseverstehen

Für das Büro Ihres Betriebs soll ein neuer Multifunktionsdrucker gekauft werden. Das Produkt Sister X5M hat es in die engere Auswahl geschafft.

Lesen Sie den Werbeprospekt auf S. 133 genau durch. Entscheiden Sie, ob die folgenden Aussagen mit Bezug auf den Prospekt richtig oder falsch sind und begründen Sie Ihre Antwort auf Deutsch. Beantworten Sie außerdem die Fragen auf Deutsch.

Aussagen		richtig	falsch
1	Wenn Sie sich für Sister X5M entscheiden, benötigen Sie vier Geräte in Ihrem Büro. *Begründung:* …	…	…
2	Sister X5M ist relativ teuer. *Begründung:* …	…	…
3	Sister X5M ist schnell und kosteneffizient. *Begründung:* …	…	…
Fragen			
4	Was lässt sich über die Druckqualität von Sister X5M sagen?		
5	Warum ist der beschriebene Drucker für eine Firma mit mehreren Büroräumen besonders gut geeignet?		
6	Wie kann man mit dem Gerät Sister X5M die Kopierkosten niedrig halten?		
7	Warum muss man weniger oft Papier nachfüllen?		
8	Inwiefern sind die Sister-Geräte umweltfreundlich? Nennen Sie drei Aspekte.		

All-in-one printers by Sister

Printing, copying, sending faxes, scanning documents … the list of tasks is endless. And so is the number of machines an office often needs to perform all of these tasks. But does it have to be this way? No! With our new all-in-one printers you need one machine only! Our newest model Sister X5M makes your dreams come true.

- Do you need a lot of space for it?
  No – Sister X5M fits in the smallest office or your home office.
- Expensive?
  Not at all – we offer the latest technology at an affordable price.
- High costs for ink cartridges or toners?
  No – our cartridges last longer than those of any other comparable printer.

Number one for efficiency

All Sister's printers offer constant printing quality: there is no difference in quality between the first print you make and number 1,000. Additionally, the printers are very fast: 16 pages per minute for coloured prints and 32 pages per minute for prints in black and white. And you can send faxes faster than ever, too.

Top for cost saving

Sister X5M saves you space and opens new opportunities for your office. On top of that you save a lot of money. Instead of having to buy three or four machines you only need one. And what is even better: the Sister X5M costs much less than four machines!
Sister X5M convinces our customers with features such as wireless and ethernet connectivity, direct USB printing and various flexible scanning options. This means that Sister X5M is network ready and allows you to save even more money because all your staff can share just one printer. If you want to reduce costs further, you can use the 'colour block feature'. This means that not everybody in the office can print in colour, but only those who have the right to do so.

Less refilling

The paper tray can be filled with 250 sheets of paper – much more than similar printers. There is a 35-sheet automatic feeder, too. Handling multi-page documents is no problem.

Go green

All our printers meet the Energy Star and Blue Angel environmental standards. Electricity consumption is low, they do not make a lot of noise and they do not heat up your office. All printers have a standby mode which helps to save energy. Forgetting to turn off the printer is a problem of the past!

For further details, please see our website at
www.sister–sisterX5M.com.

INSGESAMT 30 VP

3 **Produktion: Schriftstücke erstellen**

Ihre Ausbilderin hat Büromaterial bei einer französischen Firma bestellt, doch leider kam eine falsche Lieferung.

Sie bittet Sie, ein Beschwerdeschreiben an die französische Firma zu schicken. Schreiben Sie eine E-Mail auf Englisch mit folgendem Inhalt und achten Sie auf die korrekte Form (Betreff, Anrede, Schlussformel).

- Bezug auf die Lieferung von heute *(heutiges Datum)*; Auftragsnummer: OX41986/de.
- Es wurden statt der bestellten 100 Kugelschreiber 100 Bleistifte geliefert.
- Sie bitten um Rücknahme der Fehllieferung und sofortige Zusendung der bestellten Ware.
- Sie erwarten 20 % Rabatt, da die Kugelschreiber ein Werbegeschenk für Kunden auf einer wichtigen Messe in Bonn nächste Woche hätten sein sollen und nun zu spät ankommen werden.
- Bitten Sie um eine schnellstmögliche Antwort.

INSGESAMT 30 VP

4 **Mediation**

Ihr Vorgesetzter hat im Internet den folgenden Text gefunden, in dem Callcenter-Mitarbeitern Hinweise zum korrekten Telefonieren gegeben werden.

Er bittet Sie, auf der Grundlage dieses Textes ein Informationsblatt zum Thema ‚Regeln zum Telefonieren in unserer Firma' auf Deutsch zu erstellen. Das Informationsblatt soll bei einer Begrüßungsveranstaltung für die neuen Auszubildenden Ihrer Firma vorgestellt und verteilt werden.

TELEPHONE ETIQUETTE

Talking to customers is not always an easy thing. It can be hard to stay friendly when customers are impolite or even rude to you. But as a call centre agent you represent the company you work for and therefore you always have to stay kind and patient.

Speaking successfully means speaking clearly. Because the caller on the other end cannot see your face or body language, it is harder for him or her to understand you. Therefore, take the time to speak as clearly as you can. Also the way you talk is important. Talk slowly and try to sound happy and professional.

To be clearly understood, it is also important that you concentrate only on talking. If you eat or drink while you are talking to customers, you get distracted. Therefore: Only eat or drink during your breaks.

It is not only what you say that is important, but how you say it. Slang words and poor language are absolute no-goes. When the customer asks you a question, you should answer clearly with 'yes' or 'no'. Also you should use your normal tone of voice. Do not speak too loudly or shout!

Don't become informal and never call a customer by his or her first name. Say 'Good morning, Mr Brown.' or 'Good afternoon, Ms Sanders.'

If you work from home for a company, you should always dress as if you were at an office. The way you dress changes how you feel and how you sound. If you dress formally, you will talk more professionally. If you dress informally, you will talk like you are sitting on the couch with a friend, and the customer won't like that.

Always take the customer seriously. Show some understanding if he or she has a problem with one of the products your company sells. Repeat information back to the customer when you are taking a message to make sure you got everything right. If you are not the right person to talk to, refer the caller to a colleague who can help.

Whatever happens: Never be rude and never become unfriendly!

Mündliche Prüfung

5 Interaktion

1 Beschreiben Sie auf Englisch, wie man sich am Telefon am besten einem Kunden gegenüber verhält. Ziehen Sie zur Vorbereitung den Text auf S. 134 zu Rate.

2 Führen Sie ein Telefonat auf Englisch. Machen Sie sich dazu mit der Situation auf Ihrer Rollenkarte und den folgenden Unterlagen vertraut. Führen Sie ein möglichst freies Gespräch und gehen Sie auf die Aussagen Ihres Partners ein.

Partner A

Sie haben bei einer Firma in England Weihnachtskarten bestellt, die Sie an Ihre englischsprachigen Geschäftspartner verschicken wollen. Nach Überprüfung der Lieferung wurde festgestellt, dass die Karten nass sind und sowohl der Karton als auch die Karten auf dem Transportweg beschädigt wurden. Außerdem befindet sich auf den Karten ein anderes Bild als das bestellte.

Rufen Sie bei der Firma in England an und reklamieren Sie die Lieferung.

- Schildern Sie den Sachverhalt.
- Nennen Sie Ihre Auftragsnummer und beschreiben Sie das falsche Bild.
- Bitten Sie um schnellstmöglichen, kostenfreien Ersatz.

Partner B

Ein Kunde ruft bei Ihnen an. Führen Sie das Telefonat und reagieren Sie auf die Reklamation fachgerecht.

- Fragen Sie nach der Auftragsnummer.
- Teilen Sie dem Kunden mit, dass Sie für Transportschäden nicht verantwortlich sind.
- Vergleichen Sie die Lieferung, die der Kunde beschreibt, mit der ursprünglichen Bestellung. Sie sehen, dass ein anderes Bild als das gelieferte bestellt wurde.
- Sichern Sie eine schnelle, kostenfreie Ersatzlieferung zu, da Sie für die falsche Lieferung verantwortlich sind.

Cards&More Ltd.

8 Hackney Road – London E2 9EX
Tel. 07968 945 510, www.cardsandmore.com

ORDER NO. 8103

Article No.	Description	Quantity	Unit Price	Total Price
85201/PX/352	Christmas cards	100	£1.45	£145.00
☐	☐	☒	☐

Partner files

Situation 1.1, exercise 2A

Partner A

Sagen Sie die folgenden Sätze und lassen Sie Ihren Partner eine passende Antwort geben.

1 'I'm sorry, but Ms Schmuck couldn't come. She sent me.'
2 'Did you have a good flight?'
3 'Can I help you with your bags?'
4 'Shall we go to the car?'

Antworten Sie nun Ihrem Partner, indem Sie eine passende Antwort auswählen (eine Antwort bleibt übrig).

> No problem. • Yes, I am. • Nice to meet you, too. • Sure. • We were a bit late.

Situation 2.1, exercise 2D

Frau Kramer

- Danken Sie dem Angestellten für das interessante Meeting.
- Erklären Sie ihm, dass Sie jetzt noch zu einem Meeting in Raum 203 müssen, und bitten Sie ihn um eine Wegbeschreibung.
- Wiederholen Sie die Angaben, um sicherzugehen, dass Sie sie richtig verstanden haben.
- Bedanken und verabschieden Sie sich.

Situation 3.1, exercise 4

Partner A

- Nehmen Sie das Gespräch an.
- Stimmen Sie zu und fragen Sie, wie Sie helfen können.
- Sagen Sie, mit wem der Anrufer sprechen muss, und fragen Sie den Anrufer nach seinem Namen.
- Bitten Sie den Anrufer, seinen Namen zu buchstabieren und schreiben Sie ihn auf.
- Lesen Sie vor, was Sie aufgeschrieben haben.
- Teilen Sie dem Anrufer mit, dass Sie ihn jetzt durchstellen werden.
- Sagen Sie ‚gern geschehen'.

Situation, 3.2, exercise 2D

Partner A

- It's Susie's seventeenth birthday today.
- My landline is 01388 449355.
- Their number in France is 00 33 7718335.
- Rosa was born on 13th May 1996.
- The meeting is on 22nd February.
- Tom is on holiday until 31st May.

Partner files

FILE 5 | Situation 1.1, exercise 2A

Partner B

Antworten Sie Ihrem Partner, indem Sie eine passende Antwort auswählen (eine Antwort bleibt übrig).

> • That would be great. • Yes, I know. She sent me an e-mail. • Welcome to Munich. •
> Yes, is it this way? • Yes, it was fine.

Sagen Sie nun die folgenden Sätze und lassen Sie Ihren Partner eine passende Antwort geben.

1 'Excuse me, are you (*your partner's name*)?'
2 'Nice to meet you (*your partner's name*).'
3 'Thank you for picking me up.'
4 'Would you take this bag, please?'

FILE 6 | Situation 2.1, exercise 2D

Angestellter (in Raum 101)

- Danken Sie Frau Kramer, dass sie an dem Meeting teilgenommen hat.
- Geben Sie Frau Kramer die gewünschte Wegbeschreibung.
- Hören Sie zu, wie Frau Kramer die Angaben wiederholt; korrigieren Sie sie bei Bedarf oder bestätigen Sie, dass sie alles richtig verstanden hat.
- Reagieren Sie angemessen und verabschieden Sie sich.

FILE 7 | Situation 3.1, exercise 4

Partner B

- Bitten Sie darum, Englisch zu sprechen.
- Nennen Sie den Grund Ihres Anrufs.
- Nennen Sie Ihren Namen.
- Buchstabieren Sie Ihren Namen.
- Korrigieren Sie Partner A bei Bedarf oder bestätigen Sie, dass er Ihren Namen richtig geschrieben hat.
- Bedanken Sie sich.

FILE 8 | Situation 3.2, exercise 2D

Partner B

- Welcome to the fortieth National Games.
- The journey began on 30th June 1835.
- Mr Smith called on 21st March.
- Lena comes back on 23rd July.
- My mobile number is 07766 162833.
- Our number in the US is + 1 3566922.

Partner files

 FILE 9   ## Situation 2.1, exercise 2D

Frau Stefano

- Danken Sie dem Angestellten für das produktive Meeting.
- Erklären Sie, dass Sie jetzt noch zu einem Meeting im Raum 305 müssen, und bitten Sie um eine Wegbeschreibung.
- Wiederholen Sie die Angaben, um sicherzugehen, dass Sie sie richtig verstanden haben.
- Bedanken und verabschieden Sie sich.

 FILE 10   ## Situation 3.3, exercise 3C

Partner A

- t.smith@globalnet.co
- D.Klaus@Schwartz.com
- b.hassan76@Africa_Now.org
- R.Buchman_1986@Cornell.de

FILE 11   ## Situation 6.5, exercise 2A

Partner A

Ihr unmontierter Tisch wurde mit der folgenden Liste von Teilen und Werkzeugen geliefert, die Sie für den Zusammenbau benötigen. Verwenden Sie die unten stehenden Listen, um Ihrem Partner mitzuteilen, was geliefert worden sein sollte. Ihr Partner wird prüfen, ob jedes Teil und jedes Werkzeug vorhanden ist. Notieren Sie eventuell fehlende Teile. Beginnen Sie so: 'There should be ...'.

Thank you for buying this *Ergonomika* table.

This item has the following parts:

Item number	Item description	Quantity
ER4564	Table surface	1
T65	Table leg	4
TS3635	Screw	8
TS4545	Allen key screw	6
G2231	Leg glide	4

Tools you will need:

Screwdriver

Allen key

FILE 12 | Situation 2.1, exercise 2D

Angestellter (in Raum 206)

- Danken Sie Frau Stefano, dass sie an dem Meeting teilgenommen hat.
- Geben Sie Frau Stefano die gewünschte Wegbeschreibung.
- Hören Sie zu, wie Frau Stefano die Angaben wiederholt; korrigieren Sie sie bei Bedarf oder bestätigen Sie, dass sie alles richtig verstanden hat.
- Reagieren Sie angemessen und verabschieden Sie sich.

FILE 13 | Situation 3.3, exercise 3C

Partner B

- h.hesse@gmail.co
- k.hoffman89@Riedstadt.org
- J.Cook@Gribbon.com
- C.Hunter91@te._4_.be.co.uk

FILE 14 | Situation 6.5, exercise 2A

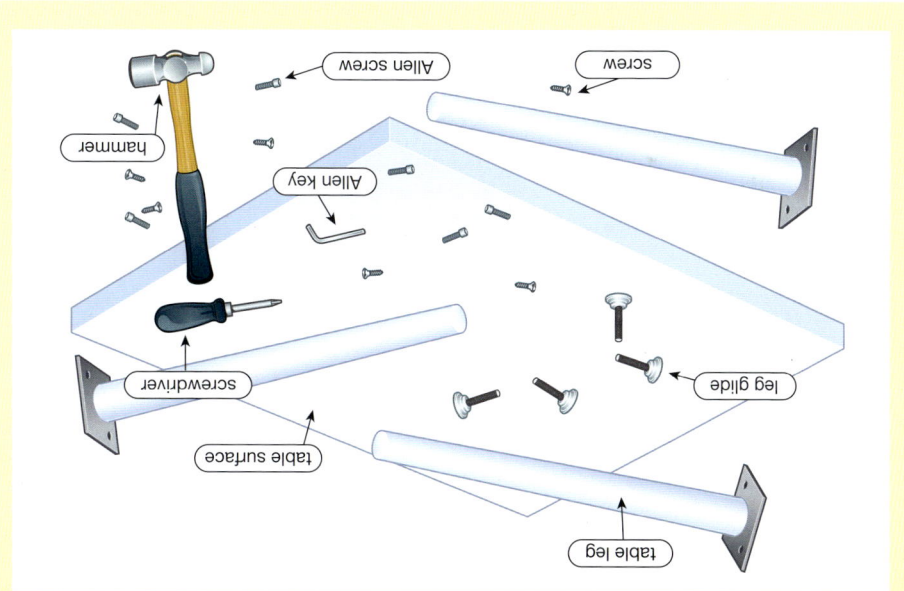

Partner B

Hier können Sie alle Einzelteile sehen, die mit der Lieferung Ihres Tisches angekommen sind, sowie die Werkzeuge, die Sie Ihrer Meinung nach brauchen werden. Ihr Partner wird Ihnen sagen, wie viele Teile jeweils vorhanden sein müssen. Prüfen Sie, ob tatsächlich alle Teile geliefert wurden und welche Werkzeuge Sie benötigen. Notieren Sie eventuell fehlende Teile. Beginnen Sie so: 'There is/are ... . One/Two/ ... is/are missing.'

Partner files

FILE 15 **Situation 11.1, exercise 3B**

Partner A

Verwenden Sie für die Terminvereinbarung den folgenden Terminkalender und bieten Sie die freien Termine an. Fangen Sie so an:

Partner A Can we make an appointment for Wednesday morning?
Partner B I'm sorry, but I can't make it then. I'm attending a … . What about Wednesday afternoon?
Partner A I'm afraid I …

Wednesday	Thursday	Friday
am *free*	am *go to an interview*	am *free*
pm *visit the warehouse*	pm *free*	pm *free*

FILE 16 **Situation 11.1, exercise 3C**

Partner A

Verwenden Sie den unten stehenden Terminkalender und vereinbaren Sie mit Ihrem Partner einen Termin für eine halbe Stunde. Das ist nicht einfach, denn Ihre Arbeitsplätze sind zwar nicht weit voneinander entfernt, aber Sie sind beide sehr beschäftigt.

Tuesday

8.30–9.00	*Meeting with the boss*
9.00–9.30	*Free*
9.30–11.00	*Study the new computer system with IT*
11.00–11.30	*Free*
11.30–12.15	*Show a visitor round the company*
12.15–1.00	*Free*
1.00–2.00	*Discuss project plans with Sales*
2.00–2.30	*Free*
2.30–4.00	*Check stocks with Production*
4.00–4.45	*Free*
4.45	*Leave the office*

FILE 17 **Situation 11.1, exercise 3B**

Partner B

Verwenden Sie zur Terminvereinbarung den folgenden Terminkalender und bieten Sie die freien Termine an. Fangen Sie so an:

Partner A Can we make an appointment for Wednesday morning?
Partner B I'm sorry, but I can't make it then. I'm attending a … . What about Wednesday afternoon?
Partner A I'm afraid I …

Wednesday	**Thursday**	**Friday**
am *attend staff meeting*	am *free*	am *go to Head Office*
pm *free*	pm *do course on safety*	pm *free*

FILE 18 **Situation 11.1, exercise 3C**

Partner B

Verwenden Sie den unten stehenden Terminkalender und vereinbaren Sie mit Ihrem Partner einen Termin für eine halbe Stunde. Das ist nicht einfach, denn Ihre Arbeitsplätze sind zwar nicht weit voneinander entfernt, aber Sie sind beide sehr beschäftigt.

Tuesday

8.30–9.30	*Prepare customer meeting*
9.30–10.30	*Meet the customer*
10.30–11.00	*Free*
11.00–12.00	*Discuss project plans with Design*
12.00–12.30	*Free*
12.30–1.30	*Have lunch with the boss*
1.30–2.15	*Free*
2.15–3.30	*Get project report ready for the boss*
3.30–3.45	*Present project report to the boss*
3.45–4.30	*Free*
4.30	*Meet a customer and then go home*

Partner files

FILE 19 **Situation 12.2, exercise 3B**

Partner A

- Laden Sie Ihren Arbeitskollegen für das kommende Wochenende in eine Bar oder ein Restaurant ein.
- Wenn Ihr Kollege ablehnt, versuchen Sie es mit einem anderen Termin.

FILE 20 **KMK exam practice, Interaktion, exercise 2**

Partner A

Sie haben gestern eine unvollständige Lieferung von einer Firma in Großbritannien bekommen. Sie hatten einen Katalog und 50 MP3-Player bestellt, aber die MP3-Player sind nicht mitgekommen. Rufen Sie bei der Firma an.

- Erklären Sie den Sachverhalt.
- Nennen Sie die Auftrags- und die Artikelnummer für die MP3-Player.
- Bitten Sie um sofortige Zusendung der fehlenden MP3-Player.
- Verhandeln Sie eine Lösung des Problems.
- Verabschieden Sie sich angemessen.

Soundwave Ltd.
28 Greenhill Road – Liverpool L1 8LW
Tel. 0151 709 3491, Fax 0151 709 3492, www.soundwave.uk

ORDER NO. 95207

Delivery address:
Peter Pan und Co. KG
Sendlingerstr. 12
86541 Kirchberg
Germany

Article No.	Description	Quantity	Unit Price	Total Price
19344/KGOTZ	mp3-players	50	€34.97	€1748.50
C/51978B	catalogue	1	€0.00	€0.00

FILE 21 — Situation 12.2, exercise 3B

Partner B

- Ihr Arbeitskollege wird Sie zum Ausgehen einladen. Erfinden Sie eine Ausrede, warum Sie nicht können.
- Versuchen Sie, den Termin mit Ihrem Kollegen zu verschieben.

FILE 22 — KMK exam practice, Interaktion, exercise 2

Soundwave Ltd.
28 Greenhill Road – Liverpool L1 8LW
Tel. 0151 709 3491, Fax 0151 709 3492, www.soundwave.uk

ORDER NO. 95207

Delivery address:
Peter Pan und Co. KG
Sendlingerstr. 12
85641 Kirchberg
Germany

Article No.	Description	Quantity	Unit Price	Total Price
19344/KG0TZ	mp3-players	50	€34.97	€1748.50
C/51978B	catalogue	1	€0.00	€0.00

Partner B

Sie erhalten einen Anruf von einem Kunden Ihrer Firma.

- Nehmen Sie den Anruf entgegen.
- Lassen Sie sich den Sachverhalt schildern.
- Bitten Sie um die Auftragsnummer und überprüfen Sie die Richtigkeit der Bestellung.
- Bestätigen Sie, dass eine Fehllieferung vorliegt.
- Finden Sie eine einvernehmliche Lösung des Problems.
- Verabschieden Sie sich angemessen.

Partner files

FILE 23 **Scenario A, Scene 3, exercise G**

Partner A

1   Stellen Sie Ihrem Partner in Ihrer Rolle als potenzieller Arbeitgeber folgende Fragen und beantworten Sie anschließend seine Fragen.

- 'Tell me about yourself.'
- 'What experience do you have?'
- 'What are your strengths and weaknesses?'
- 'Can you work weekends?'
- 'Do you have any questions for me?'

2   Beantworten Sie nun die Fragen Ihres Partners und stellen Sie ihm in Ihrer Rolle als Bewerber folgende Fragen.

- 'What training will you give me?'
- 'Can you tell me what a typical work week is like?'
- 'What will my responsibilities be?'

FILE 24 **Scenario D, Scene 2, exercise B**

Eric/Erica Hoffman (from SonnenPower)

- You now know that SonnenPower can:
  - deliver the panels that Etoile Construction needs by the 15th;
  - send a team to install the panels by the same date (because a job in the UK is going to finish early).
- You call Pierre/Perrine Bertrand back to give him/her this information.
- When Pierre/Perrine says how happy he/she is, you tell him/her that SonnenPower always tries to help its customers as much as possible.

FILE 25 **Scenario D, Scene 4, exercise A**

Paul's information

POSSIBLE FLIGHTS

Time	Cost (single)	Flight no.
10.35 a.m.	£58.99	EJ5325
3.25 p.m.	£69.99	BR2796
6.50 p.m.	£76.50	RA462

FILE 26 · Scenario A, Scene 3, exercise G

Partner B

1 **Beantworten Sie die Fragen Ihres Partners und stellen Sie ihm anschließend in Ihrer Rolle als Bewerber folgende Fragen.**

- 'What training will you give me?'
- 'Can you tell me what a typical work week is like?'
- 'What will my responsibilities be?'

2 **Stellen Sie nun Ihrem Partner in Ihrer Rolle als potenzieller Arbeitgeber die folgenden Fragen und beantworten Sie seine.**

- 'What qualifications do you have?'
- 'What are your hobbies?'
- 'Do you have a driving licence?'
- 'Where do you want to be in five years?'
- 'Do you have any questions for me?'

FILE 27 · Scenario D, Scene 2, exercise B

Pierre/Perrine Bertrand (from Étoile)

- You are glad to hear from Eric/Erica Hoffman, but you are very worried.
- Tell him/her again that you really need the panels next week.
- You are happy to hear that SonnenPower can deliver on the 15th, but you are still worried: delivering the panels is one thing, but installing them is another.
- You are very happy when Eric/Erica tells you that Sonnenpower can also send a team to do the job at the start of next week.

FILE 28 · Scenario D, Scene 4, exercise A

Turgut's information

TRAVEL TO THE AIRPORT

By:	Travel time:	Cost:		Changes:
Bus	2hr 30min	£27.00 × 5 = £135.00		1 (taxi → bus)
		+		
		£15.00		
		£150.00		
Train	2hr 10min	£24.00 × 5 = £120.00		3 (taxi → train 1 → train 2 → train 3)
		+		
		£15.00		
		£135.00		
Taxi	2hr 30min	£140.00		0

FILE 29 **Scenario C, Scene 5, exercise B**

Jonathan Green
Photo Designer

432 Main Street, Guilford, UK, GU34 3ED

Phone 0463 2628736
E-mail j.g_reen@photodesign.co.uk

GG
Krakow

Wojtek Marclewski
Programmer

+48 12 37268 84
wojtek.marcelwski@gg.pl

Sven
Henriksen
Assistant carer

 +46 8 3746 4637

 sven.carer@homehelp.se

Blue Pool
Washing
Machines

Lauren Barton
Technician

2312 Albany Drive, Alexandria
Virginia, USA

lauren_barton.12@bluepool.com

NETTI

Valentina Nardi
ASSISTANT MANAGER

Via Andrea Giacinto 5, 31352 Venice, Italy
ag.venice@netti.it

Future Films GmbH

Marcel Müller
Assistant Director

Berlin, Germany

Mobile
+49 7675 76482239

Ivan Sauvage
Real Estate Manager

Aix-en-Provence, France
+33(0)438297045
i.sauv@prov-est.fr

PROVENCE ESTATES

TALLER DE TAPAS

Maria Mendez
Chef

Plaza Santa Isabella, 4, Barcelona
Tel: 093 289 39 23

IRELAND

Jennifer Robinson
Java Programmer

jrobinson-java@intelli.ie

Zoe Manetas
Hairdresser

Undercut Hair Salon

Odysseos 12, Athens 10444, Greece
Tel: +30 210 7645 2398
E-mail: info@undercut-hair.gr

Alphabetisches Wörterverzeichnis

Dieses Wörterverzeichnis enthält alle neuen Wörter aus *Job Basics A2* in alphabetischer Reihenfolge. Nicht angeführt sind Wörter, die zum Grundwortschatz *(Basic word list)* gehören. Die Zahl nach dem Stichwort bezieht sich auf die Seite, auf der das Wort zum ersten Mal erscheint. Wörter aus den Hörverständnis-übungen sind zusätzlich mit einem **T** (Transkript) und Wörter aus den *Partner files* mit einem **P** gekennzeichnet. Wörter, die zum fortgeschrittenen Wortschatz *(Advanced word list)* gehören, sind mit einem **+** gekennzeichnet. Diese Wörter sind schon auf den Seiten, auf denen sie erscheinen, übersetzt.

electricity *102* Strom, Elektrizität
to e-mail *50T* mailen, eine E-Mail schreiben
emergency *28* Notfall
emergency exit *102* Notausgang
emotion *72T* Gefühl, Emotion
empathy *95* Einfühlungsvermögen
to employ *54T* beschäftigen
employee *49* Angestellte/r, Beschäftigte/r, Mitarbeiter/in
employer *70* Arbeitgeber
employment agency *66+* Arbeitsvermittlung
to empty *64* leeren
en suite *120* mit Bad/Dusche und WC
enclosed *94* beigefügt, beiliegend
endless *133* unendlich
engineering *10* Maschinenbau
enclosures *94* (Brief:) Anlagen
to enquire about sth *114* sich nach etw erkundigen
enquiry *40* Anfrage
to enter sth *11T* etw betreten, in etw hineinkommen; ~ (data) *49* (Daten) eingeben
entire *75* ganz, gesamt, komplett
entrance *8* Eingang; goods ~ *10T* Wareneingang; main ~ *14* Haupteingang
environment *52* Umwelt; work ~ *67* Arbeitsumgebung, -umfeld
environmental *133* Umwelt-
equipment *14T* Geräte, Ausstattung; *26* Ausrüstung; specialist ~ *97T* Spezialausstattung, -ausrüstung
ergonomic *72* ergonomisch
escalator *12T* Rolltreppe
especially *11T* besonders, insbesondere
estate, industrial ~ *18* Gewerbegebiet
ethnic *86* ethnisch
etiquette *134* Etikette, Umgangsformen
even more so *75* (und) erst recht
evening class *92* Abendschule
evenly *60* gleichmäßig
event *21* Veranstaltung; *122* Ereignis
excellent *10T* ausgezeichnet, hervorragend
exciting *34T* spannend, aufregend
exclamation mark *114* Ausrufezeichen
excrement *72T* Kot, Exkrement(e)
exhibition *109* Ausstellung, Messe
exhibitor *21T* Aussteller
existing *49* (bereits) bestehend
exit *16* Ausgang
to exit sth *17* etw verlassen
experience *30* Erfahrung
expert *36T* Fachmann/-frau, Experte/-in
to explain *10* erklären, erläutern
expression *127* Ausdruck
extension *39* (Telefon:) Durchwahl, Anschluss
external *22* extern

extreme *72* extrem
extremely *131* äußerst

F
face mask *66* Gesichtsmaske, Atemmaske
fact, in ~ *50T* eigentlich, genau genommen, tatsächlich
factory *10T* Fabrik, Werk
fair *21T* Messe
false *96* falsch
family-run *120* in Familienbesitz
fancy *116+* extravagant, schick, nobel
fantastic *52* fantastisch, toll
farm *72* Bauernhof, Farm
fashion *110* Mode
feature *52+* Eigenschaft, Merkmal, Besonderheit
feeder *133* (Papier-)Zufuhr
to feel comfortable *129* sich wohlfühlen
field *92* Feld, Bereich
file *105+* Datei
to fill sth out *98* etw ausfüllen
finally *60* schließlich, zuletzt
finance controller *31T* Rechnungsprüfer/in, Controller/in
financial *86* Finanz-
to finish *10* enden, zu Ende gehen; ~ sth *31T* etw abschließen
finished goods *10T* fertige Ware
fire *34T* Feuer, Kaminfeuer; by the ~ *34T* am Kamin
firm *86* Firma
first aid *32* Erste Hilfe
first name *86* Vorname
first of all *106T* zuallererst, zunächst
first-aid kit *102* Verbandkasten
to fit in *130* dazu passen, sich einfügen; ~ in sth *133* in etw hineinpassen
flat *28* Wohnung
flexibility *62* Flexibilität
flexible *30* flexibel
flight *6* Flug
flood *83* Überschwemmung
floor manager *76+* Abteilungsleiter/in
flower *51* Blume, Blüte
to fold *89* falten
follow, as ~s *100* wie folgt, folgendermaßen
follow-up *114* Folge-, Nachfass-
foot, on ~ *16* zu Fuß
for hire *28* zu mieten
for now *27T* einstweilen, fürs Erste
for sale *51* zu verkaufen
for short *108T* kurz
force, storm ~ *27T* Windstärke
foreign *68* fremd, Fremd-, ausländisch
foreign country *68* Ausland
foreign language *32* Fremdsprache
foreigner *131+* Ausländer/in
forest *113T* Wald
fork *19T* Gabelung
formal *88* formell, förmlich
formula 1 *54T* Formel 1
to forward *39* weiterleiten
free *62* kostenlos
freezer *65* Gefrierschrank
frequently *105* häufig
fresh *72T* frisch

fridge *65* Kühlschrank
fried potatoes *61* Bratkartoffeln
friend, to make ~s *109* Freunde gewinnen
fruit *64* Frucht, Früchte, Obst
frustrating *72T* frustrierend
to fry *60* braten
frying pan *60* Bratpfanne
fuel-efficient *40+* Kraftstoff sparend
fumes *72T* Dämpfe
fun *51* Spaß; amüsant, lustig
function *39* Funktion
further *68* weitere/e/s
further away *131* weiter weg

G
gap *21T* Lücke
gastronomy *30* Gastronomie
gate *101T* Tor
gender *86* Geschlecht
general *68* allgemein
to get back to sb *27T* jdn zurückrufen, sich bei jdm melden
to get distracted *134* abgelenkt werden
to get hurt *70* sich verletzen
to get married *50T* heiraten
to get rid of sth *104+* etw loswerden
to get started *59* anfangen, loslegen
to get through *27* durchkommen
to give up *92* aufgeben
to give directions *13* den Weg beschreiben/erklären
to give a result *52* ein Ergebnis liefern
to give a speech *88* eine Rede halten
glassware *77* Glas, Glaswaren
gloves *66* Handschuhe
to go ahead *22T* anfangen, loslegen, weitermachen
to go along (the corridor) *12T* (den Gang) entlang gehen
to go on *25T* dauern
goodbye, to say ~ *131* sich verabschieden
Goodbye for now. *27T* Bis dann!
goodbye party *122* Abschiedsparty
goods *10T* Ware(n); finished ~ *10T* fertige Ware; ~ entrance *10T* Wareneingang; ~ exit *11* Warenausgang
Gosh! *34T* Meine Güte!
grade *32* Klasse(nstufe)
gram *52* Gramm
to grate *60* reiben
grave *88+* Grab
to grease *60+* einfetten
to greet sb *8* jdn begrüßen
greeting *88* Begrüßung
grey *44T* grau
ground floor *101* Erdgeschoss
guideline *114* Richtlinie
gym *110+* Fitnessstudio

H
hair salon *32T* Friseursalon
hairdresser *32T* Friseur/in
hairdressing *32* Friseurhandwerk
handbag *19T* Handtasche
handle *52* Griff
to handle sth *41* mit etw umgehen, mit etw fertig werden

to hang sth *63* etw aufhängen; ~ up *27T* (Telefon:) auflegen; ~ sth up *8* etw aufhängen
to happen *64* geschehen, passieren; to make sth ~ *64* etw umsetzen
hard hat *66* Schutzhelm
hard-working *30* fleißig
to hate *31T* hassen, überhaupt nicht mögen
Have a seat. *97T* Nehmen Sie Platz!
hazard *70* Gefahr
hazardous substance *72* Gefahrstoff, Gefahrenstoff
headline *51* Überschrift
headquarters *54+* Zentrale, Firmensitz
health *14* Gesundheit
health care *72* Gesundheitswesen
health centre *14* Gesundheitszentrum
Health & Safety *70* Arbeitsschutz, Arbeitssicherheit
heart *14* Herz
to heat *60* erhitzen; ~ sth up *133* etw aufheizen
heavy *103T* schwer
height *44* Höhe
helpful *21T* nützlich, dienlich
to hesitate *71* zögern
to hide *39* verbergen; *122* sich verstecken
high *35* Höchstwert
high-quality *42T* hochwertig
high-visibility jacket *66* Warnweste
high voltage *102* Hochspannung
higher education *33* Hochschulbildung
to highlight *105* hervorheben, betonen
to hike *113T* wandern
hill *16* Hügel, Anhöhe
to hire sb *75* jdn einstellen, jdn anstellen
hire, for ~ *28* zu mieten
history *54* Geschichte
hole *63* Loch
to hold *48* (aus)halten, tragen; ~ (the line) *23* (Telefon:) am Apparat bleiben
hold, to put sb/a call on ~ *39* jdn/einen Anruf in die Warteschleife legen
holiday, on ~ *8* im Urlaub
holographic *115* holografisch
home care *28* ambulante/ häusliche Pflege
home town *36* Heimatstadt
homeland *131* Heimatland
home-stay family *108T* Gastfamilie
honest *92* ehrlich, aufrichtig
honey *126* Honig
hospital *18* Krankenhaus
host *7* Gastgeber
hour, to work long ~s *30* lange/ bis spät arbeiten
household goods *76* Haushaltswaren, -artikel
Human Resources (HR) *10T* Personalabteilung
humour *99T* Humor
to hurt *72T* wehtun; ~ sb *72T* jdn verletzen; ~ sth *69* sich etw verletzen
hurt, to get ~ *70* sich verletzen

neck *72T* Hals
neighbour *125* Nachbar/in
nervous *98* nervös
network *54* Netzwerk
next to *39* neben
Nice to meet you. *6T* Schön, Sie kennen zu lernen.
night, at ~ *64* abends
noise *72* Lärm
noisy *93* laut, lärmend
none *49* keine/r/s
noodle *60* Nudel
not … either *31T* auch nicht
not … until *10* nicht vor …, erst
to not care *50T* egal sein
to note *24* notieren, aufschreiben
note, thank-you ~ *75* Dankesschreiben; to take ~s *75* sich Notizen machen
notice *64* Mitteilung, Aushang. Bekanntmachung
to notice *64* bemerken, auffallen
now, for ~ *27T* einstweilen, fürs Erste
nurse *78* Krankenschwester/-pfleger
nursing *97T* Pflege, Krankenpflege
nut *60* Nuss

O

occasionally *60* gelegentlich
of all time *54T* aller Zeiten
off, to take some time ~ *73T* sich frei nehmen
offensive *86+* anstößig
office administration, qualification in ~ *31* Abschluss als Bürokaufmann/-frau
office equipment *10T* Bürobedarf, Büromaterial
Office Services *10T* Verwaltungsdienste
official *109* offiziell
off-road *40+* geländegängig
olive oil *60* Olivenöl
on foot *16* zu Fuß
on holiday *8* im Urlaub
on site *116T* vor Ort
on the beach *34T* am Strand
on time *6* pünktlich
on top of *48* (oben) auf
on weekdays *29* wochentags, werktags
one by one *104+* nacheinander, einzeln, eins nach dem anderen
one-way ticket *119T* einfache Fahrt, Hinfahrt/-flug
onion *60* Zwiebel
on-the-job training *96* Ausbildung am Arbeitsplatz, innerbetriebliche Ausbildung
opening *109* Eröffnung
to operate *67* tätig sein, arbeiten, operieren
operating system *52+* Betriebssystem
operations *100* Geschäftstätigkeit(en)
opinion *115* Meinung
opportunity *133* Möglichkeit, Gelegenheit
to optimize *50T+* optimieren
order *25T* Bestellung, Auftrag
order, in ~ *14T* in Ordnung
order form *82* Bestellformular, Auftragsformular

ordinary *129+* gewöhnlich, alltäglich
organiser *109* Organisator/in
organized *95* (gut) organisiert
…-oriented *95* …-orientiert
otherwise *6T* sonst, ansonsten
outdoors *30* draußen, im Freien
outgoing *30+* kontaktfreudig, aufgeschlossen
output *52* Leistung, Ausstoß
to outsource *49* auslagern, (ins Ausland) verlagern
overall *54T* insgesamt
to overfill *65* überfüllen
overview *54* Überblick
owner *97* Inhaber/in, Besitzer/in

P

package *60* Packung, Päckchen
packaging *62* Verpackung
packed lunch *120* Lunchpaket
packing *14T* Verpackung
pain *19T* Schmerz(en); to be in ~ *19T* Schmerzen haben
pain-killer *19T* Schmerzmittel
pan *60* Topf, Pfanne
pancake *61* Pfannkuchen
paper tray *58* Papierfach
paperwork *14T* Unterlagen, Papiere; *98* Büroarbeit, Formalitäten
paragraph *98* (Text:) Absatz
part, to take ~ in sth *21T* an etw teilnehmen
part time *31* Teilzeit
particular, in ~ *67* besonders, speziell, insbesondere
to pass sth on *128* etw weitergeben
passenger *21T* Fahrgast, Passagier
passport *96* Pass
past *133* Vergangenheit
past … *10T* an … vorbei
path *101* Weg
patience *21T* Geduld
patient *78* Patient/in; *84T* geduldig
to pay attention to sth *71* auf etw achten, einer Sache Aufmerksamkeit schenken
to peel *60+* schälen
pen *9* Stift
percent *131* Prozent
to perform sth *133* etw ausführen
perfume *75* Parfum
period (of time) *30* Zeitabschnitt, Zeitraum
personality *30+* Persönlichkeit
petrol station *18* Tankstelle
pharmacy *18* Apotheke
photocopier *58* Fotokopierer/-kopiergerät
physical *72* körperlich, physisch
piano *40* Klavier
to pick up *6T* abholen; *23T* (Telefon:) ans Telefon gehen, abheben
pity, a ~ *68* schade
to place *58* platzieren, legen, setzen, stellen; ~ sb *108T* jdn vermitteln
place, to take ~ *75* stattfinden
placement, work ~ *84* Praktikum
plain *60* einfach
plate *60* Teller, Platte
platform *21T* Bahnsteig

Pleased to meet you. *36T* Erfreut, Sie kennen zu lernen.
pleasure, My ~. *96T* Gern geschehen.
to plug sth in *46+* etw einstecken
plug, wall ~ *62* Dübel
pocket *88* (Hosen-, Jacken-) Tasche
point, You've got a ~. *125* Da hast du recht.
poison *71* Gift
police station *16* Polizeiwache
Polish *84T* polnisch
polite *36* höflich
politics *129* Politik
pond *16* Teich
popular *41* beliebt
population *115+* Bevölkerung, Einwohner
pork *60* Schweinefleisch
porter *110T* Gepäckträger, Portier
position *75* Stelle
possible *21T* möglich
to post *96* (ab)schicken
poster *50T* Plakat
pot *60* Topf
potato *61* Kartoffel; fried ~es *61* Bratkartoffeln
potential *36* möglich, potenziell
to pour *60* schütten, gießen
powder *60* Pulver
power *53* Leistung; *62* Kraft, Energie; *64* Strom
power drill *62* Bohrmaschine
power output *52+* (elektrische) Leistung
power tool *62* Elektrowerkzeug
to prefer *34T* vorziehen, lieber mögen
to prepare *62* vorbereiten, ausarbeiten, erstellen
to prepare food *124* Essen zubereiten, kochen
prepared *68* bereit
to press *39* drücken
to pretend *111* so tun, als ob
previous *114* vorig, vorhergehend
price list *26* Preisliste
primary school *32* Grundschule
print *133* Ausdruck
to print *42* drucken
printer *42* Drucker
printing quality *133* Druckqualität
probable *126* wahrscheinlich
product launch *51* Produkteinführung
product line *44* Produktlinie
product range *106* Produktpalette, Sortiment
production director *89* Produktionsleiter/in
production hall *10T* Produktionshalle, Fertigungshalle
profession *28* Beruf
professional *75* berufsbezogen, professionell
professional group *95* Berufsgruppe
programmer *113P* Programmierer/in
promotion *86+* Beförderung, Aufstieg
to pronounce *128* aussprechen
proper(ly) *46* richtig
to protect *86* schützen

protection *73T* Schutz; ear ~ *73T* Gehörschutz
protective clothing *73T* Schutzkleidung
to provide sth *67+* etw zur Verfügung stellen
psychological *72* psychologisch
the public *28* die Öffentlichkeit
purchasing (department) *76+* Einkauf(sabteilung)
purchasing manager *10* Einkaufsleiter/in
purpose *44* Zweck; *105T* Absicht
to put *87* formulieren; ~ sth up *50T* etw aufhängen; *70* etw aufstellen
to put sb through *23* (Telefon:) jdn durchstellen
to put sb/a call on hold *39* jdn/ einen Anruf in die Warteschleife legen

Q

qualification *28* Abschluss, Qualifikation, Ausbildung
qualification in office administration *31* Abschluss als Bürokaufmann/-frau
quality, high-~ *42T* hochwertig
quantity *49P* Menge

R

racer *54* Rennwagen
railway *18* Eisenbahn
railway station *119T* Bahnhof
range, product ~ *106* Produktpalette, Sortiment
rated *52* bewertet, eingestuft
rating *42* Bewertung
to reach *83* erreichen
to read sth back to sb *24T* etw (für jdn) wiederholen, jdm etw vorlesen
real estate *113P* Immobilien
to realize *50T* auffallen, bemerken, klar werden
reason *122* Grund, Anlass
to receive *10* erhalten, bekommen
receiver *39* (Telefon:) Hörer
reception *10* Rezeption, Empfang
receptionist *79* Empfangsmitarbeiter/in
recipe *60* (Koch-)Rezept
recipient *39* Empfänger/in
to recommend *36* empfehlen
recommendation *30+* Empfehlung
to record *22* aufzeichnen
to reduce *133* senken, reduzieren
to refer sb to sb *134* jdn an jdn verweisen, jdn an jdn weiterleiten
to refill *133* nachfüllen, auffüllen
to refuse *88* ablehnen, verweigern
regard, Best ~s, *40* (Brief:) Mit freundlichen Grüßen
regular train *21T* fahrplanmäßiger Zug
to relax *75* sich entspannen
relaxed *75* locker, entspannt
relevant *95* wichtig, relevant
remaining *91T* übrig
to remove *96* entfernen
repair *28* Reparatur
reply *117* Antwort

to reply (to sth) *41* (auf etw) antworten

representative *49* Vertreter/in

reputation *86* Ruf

request *8* Bitte, Anfrage; *68* Aufforderung

requirement *30* Anforderung

requirement *66+* Anforderung, Vorschrift, Bestimmung

research *88* Nachforschungen, Recherche; **to do ~** *88* Nachforschungen anstellen, recherchieren

Research & Development (R & D) *10* Forschung und Entwicklung(sabteilung)

reservation *78* Reservierung

resident *95* Bewohner/in

respectful *122* respektvoll

to respond to sth *82* auf etw reagieren, auf etw antworten

responsibility *97T* Aufgabe, Verantwortlichkeit

responsible *93* verantwortungsbewusst; **to be ~ for sth** *108T* für etw zuständig/verantwortlich sein

resources *64+* Ressourcen

result *52* Ergebnis; **as a ~** *78* daher, deshalb; **to give a ~** *52* ein Ergebnis liefern

retail *42* Einzelhandel

retail assistant *42* Einzelhandelskaufman/-frau, Verkäufer/in

to retire *122* sich zur Ruhe setzen, in Rente gehen

rice *61* Reis

rid, to get ~ of sth *104+* etw loswerden

right away *70* sofort, umgehend

Romanian *84T* rumänisch

roof *116T* Dach

room, double ~ *79* Doppelzimmer; **single ~** *79* Einzelzimmer

round the corner *10T* um die Ecke

roundabout *14T* Kreisverkehr

rubber *52* Gummi

rubbish *64* Abfall, Müll

rubbish bin *64+* Mülleimer

rude *84T* unhöflich, unverschämt

rule *64* Regel, Vorschrift

to run late *80* zu spät (dran) sein; *86* lange dauern

S

sad *72T* traurig

sadness *88* Traurigkeit

safe(ly) *41* sicher

safety *30* (Arbeits-)Sicherheit; **Health & S~** *70* Arbeitsschutz, Arbeitssicherheit

safety boots *66* Sicherheitsstiefel/-schuhe

safety measure *91* Sicherheitsmaßnahme

sailing *109* Segeln

salad *61* Salat

sale *51* Verkauf; **for ~** *51* zu verkaufen

sales *10* Verkauf, Vertrieb; *83* Verkäufe, Umsatz

sales assistant *44* Verkäufer/in

sales representative (rep.) *76+* Vertreter/in

to sand *52* schleifen

sander *52* Schleifmaschine, Schleifer

sauce *60* Soße

sausage *84* Wurst, Würstchen

to save *39* sichern, speichern

to say goodbye *131* sich verabschieden

to scan (a text) *131* (einen Text) überfliegen

scary *92* furchteinflößend, unheimlich

schedule *72* Zeitplan, Terminplan

school leaving certificate *32* Abschlusszeugnis, Schulabschluss

scientist *130* Naturwissenschaftler/in, Forscher/in

scooter *40* Motorroller

scrambled eggs *61* Rührei(er)

to scrape out *46+* herauskratzen

screw *49P* Schraube; **to drive a ~** *62* eine Schraube eindrehen

screwdriver *49P* Schraubenzieher, -dreher

sea star *26* Seestern

seafood *126* Meeresfrüchte

seat *97T* Sitz, Platz; **Have a ~.** *97T* Nehmen Sie Platz!

secondary school *33* weiterführende Schule

secondly *125* zweitens

sector *95* Sektor

secure *121* sicher

security *14* Sicherheit

security officer *14* Sicherheitsbeauftragte/r

see-through *63* durchsichtig

to seem *19T* scheinen

to select *39* auswählen, wählen

separate(ly) *128* einzeln

serious *99* ernst, ernsthaft

seriously, to take sb/sth ~ *134* jdn/etw ernst nehmen

to serve *36T* servieren

serving *60* Portion

to set up *39* einrichten, einstellen; *86* aufbauen

to shake hands *88* die Hand schütteln, die Hand geben

shall *6T* sollen

to share *123T* (sich etw) teilen, mitteilen

sheet *42* Blatt (Papier)

sheet metal *21T* Blech

shift *95* Schicht

shirt *67* Hemd

shock *69* Schock

shoe laces *111T* Schnürsenkel

shopkeeper *72* Geschäftsinhaber/in, Ladenbesitzer/in

shopper *18* jd, der einkaufen geht

shopping centre *18* Einkaufszentrum

short, for ~ *108T* kurz

short cut *16* Abkürzung

short notice *77* kurzfristig

to shout *122* rufen

to show sb around *9* jdn herumführen

shower *35* (Regen-)Schauer; *120* Dusche

sick *72T* krank

sightseeing *84* Besichtigungen machen

sign *70* Schild, Hinweis

silent(ly) *102* still, stumm

silly *99+* albern

similar *52* ähnlich

sincerely, Yours ~ *16* (Brief:) Mit freundlichen Grüßen

singer *84* Sänger/in

single room *79* Einzelzimmer

to sit back *119T* sich zurücklehnen

site, industrial ~ *14* Betriebsgelände, Industriestandort; **on ~** *116T* vor Ort

size *58* Größe

to ski *34T* Ski fahren/laufen

skiing *34T* Skifahren/-laufen

skill *11T* Fähigkeit, Fertigkeit, Kenntnisse

to skim (a text) *115* (einen Text) überfliegen

skin *71* Haut

skirt *67* Rock

to slide *52* gleiten

slight *10T* klein; *88* leicht

to slip *63* abrutschen; ausrutschen

smart *41* schlau, schick, elegant, pfiffig

to smell *72T* riechen

to smile *86* lächeln

snow *34* Schnee

to snow *34* schneien

social *54* sozial, gesellschaftlich

soft *52* weich

solar energy *8* Sonnen-/ Solarenergie

solar panel *116T* Solarmodul

solid *42* fest, solide

solution *46* Lösung

to solve *122* lösen

sort *62* Art

to sort *127* sortieren, einordnen, gruppieren

sound system *124* Beschallungsanlage

soup *61* Suppe

to speak up *27T* lauter sprechen

specialist equipment *97T* Spezialausstattung, -ausrüstung

specialized *95* Spezial-, spezialisiert

specific *50T* speziell, spezifisch

specification, technical ~s *26* technische Daten

speech *88* Rede; **to give a ~** *88* eine Rede halten

speed *42* Geschwindigkeit; *62* (Schaltgetriebe:) Gang

spellchecker *105* Rechtschreibüberprüfung

spelling *105* Rechtschreibung

spoken *6* gesprochen

spout *46* Auslauf, Ausguss

spring *34* Frühling

spur *41* Sporn

square *60* Quadrat, Rechteck; *60* quadratisch, rechteckig

staff *14* Personal, Mitarbeiter

staff car *97T* Dienstwagen

staff member *106* Mitarbeiter/ in, Angestellte/r

stairs *101* Treppe

standard *133* Norm; **to meet a ~** *133* eine Norm erfüllen

standby *133* Bereitschaft

star *42T* Stern

starter *126* Vorspeise

statement *96* Aussage, Behauptung

statistics *131* Statistik

steam *52* Dampf

steel *36T* Stahl

step *71* (Treppen-)Stufe; *92* Schritt

sterile *67* steril

to stir *60+* rühren

stir-fry *61* pfannengerührt, kurz gebraten

storage *14* Lagerung

storage room *68* Lager(raum)

store *111* Laden, Geschäft

storm force *27T* Windstärke

straight *10T* direkt, sofort

straight ahead *19T* geradezu, geradeaus

straight on *14T* geradeaus

to strain *10* abgießen

strength *97T* Stärke

stressful *116* anstrengend, stressig

strong *92* stark

to study sth *102* sich etw genau ansehen

stylish *41* elegant, stilvoll, modisch

subject line *105T* Betreffzeile

substance *72+* Stoff, Subtanz; **hazardous ~** *72* Gefahrstoff, Gefahrenstoff

successful *30* erfolgreich

sudden *116* plötzlich

suddenly *83* plötzlich

sugar *60* Zucker

to suggest *41* vorschlagen

suggestion *91T* Vorschlag

suit *86* Anzug (Herren), Hosenanzug (Damen)

suitable *40* geeignet, passend

suitcase *112* Koffer

suite, en ~ *120* mit Bad/Dusche und WC

summary *119* Zusammenfassung

summer job *30* Ferienjob

sunflower *60* Sonnenblume

sunny *34T* sonnig

supermarket *16* Supermarkt

supplier *26* Lieferant, Zulieferer

supplies *61* Vorräte

to support *34+* unterstützen, Fan sein von

to suppose *10T* annehmen, vermuten

sure, to make ~ *75* dafür sorgen, sicherstellen

surface *52+* Oberfläche, Fläche; **table ~** *49P* Tischplatte

surfboard *27T* Surfbrett

surgery *78* (Arzt-)Praxis

surname *84T* Nachname

to surprise *86* überraschen, erstaunen

to survive *75* überleben

sweet *3* Süßigkeit

to switch sth on/off *64* etw ein-/ausschalten

swivel chair *44* Drehstuhl

T

table surface *49P* Tischplatte

tablespoon *60* Esslöffel

to take over *103* übernehmen

to take part in sth *21T* an etw teilnehmen

to take place *75* stattfinden

to take sb/sth seriously *134* jdn/etw ernst nehmen

to take time *92* Zeit brauchen, (lange) dauern

to take some time off *73T* sich frei nehmen

to take a break *73T* eine Pause machen, eine Auszeit nehmen
to take criticism *95* Kritik annehmen
to take a message *24* (jdm) etw ausrichten
to take notes *75* sich Notizen machen
talk *84* Vortrag
tape *63* Band, Klebeband
target *122+* Ziel, Zielvorgabe
to taste sth *109* etw versuchen, etw probieren
tasty *84* lecker, schmackhaft
tax *99+* Steuer
team leader *117* Gruppenleiter/in
teaspoon *60* Teelöffel
technical *26* technisch
technical specifications *26* technische Daten
technician *8* Techniker/in
technology *28* Technik, Technologie
temperature *71* Temperatur
terrible *6T* furchtbar, fürchterlich
text message *17* SMS
thank-you note *75* Dankesschreiben
theatre *109* Theater
theme *126* Motto
therefore *134* deshalb
to think about sth *75* über etw nachdenken
this way *6T* hier entlang
though *34T* aber, allerdings
thunderstorm *34* Gewitter
tidy *64* ordentlich, aufgeräumt
to tidy up *64* aufräumen
tie *66* Krawatte
tile, ceramic ~ *62* Keramikfliese
till (= until) *10* bis
time, of all ~ *54T* aller Zeiten
time, on ~ *6* pünktlich
time, part ~ *31* Teilzeit
time, to take ~ *92* Zeit brauchen, (lange) dauern
time, to take some ~ off *73T* sich frei nehmen
time, waste of ~ *99T* Zeitverschwendung
time difference *21T* Zeitverschiebung
timesheet *64+* Stundennachweis
timetable *99T* Fahrplan; *100* Stundenplan
T-intersection *19T* Einmündung
tip *30+* Trinkgeld
titanium *36T* Titan *(Metall)*
title *84T* Titel; **job ~** *29* Berufsbezeichnung
tomato *61* Tomate
tone of voice *134* Tonfall
tongue, mother ~ *96T* Muttersprache
tonne *41* Tonne
tool *49P* Werkzeug
top quality *51* hochwertig, erstklassig

topic *37* Thema
tough *92* zäh
tour *10* Rundgang
tour guide *40* Reiseführer/in
toxic *102* giftig
top, on ~ of *48* (oben) auf
track *21T* Gleis
to trade sth *113* etw austauschen
trade fair *26* Handelsmesse, Fachmesse
traffic *119T* Verkehr
traffic jam *80* Stau
traffic lights *18* Verkehrsampel
train station *6* Bahnhof
trainee *26* Auszubildende/r
to train *93* schulen, ausbilden; *97T* ausgebildet werden, eine Ausbildung machen
training *10* Ausbildung, Schulung; **on-the-job ~** *96* Ausbildung am Arbeitsplatz, innerbetriebliche Ausbildung
training manager *64* Ausbildungsleiter/in
to transfer *22* weiterleiten, *(Telefon:)* durchstellen
to translate *80* übersetzen
transport Transport, Beförderung
to transport *41* transportieren, befördern
travel agent *119* Reisebüro, Reiseverkehrskaufmann/-frau
traveller *80* Reisende/r
tray *48* Tablett; **paper ~** *58* Papierfach
to treat *86+* behandeln
triple *44* dreifach
trousers *67* Hose
truck *14* Lastwagen
truck driver *14* Lastwagenfahrer/in
trust *115* Vertrauen
tuna *126* Thunfisch
to turn *46* drehen; **~ left/right** *12T* links/rechts abbiegen
to turn sth into sth *82* etw aus etw machen
to turn sth off *64* etw ausschalten
to turn sth on *58* etw einschalten
TV show *54* Fernsehsendung
to type *50T* *(Text)* eintippen, eingeben
typical *97* typisch
typically *75* normalerweise

U

umbrella *88* Regenschirm
uncomfortable *72+* unbequem
underscore *27* Unterstrich
understanding *134* Verständnis
unemployed *122* arbeitslos
unfortunately *68* unglücklicherweise, leider
unhappy *72* unzufrieden
unimportant *129* unwichtig
unit price *135* Einzelpreis, Stückpreis

United Arab Emirates *66* Vereinigte arabische Emirate
universe *52* Universum
university *33* Universität
untidy *64* unaufgeräumt
until, not … ~ *10* nicht vor …, erst
up, What's ~? *114* Wie geht's? Alles klar?
uppercase *27* (in) Großbuchstaben
upstairs *12T* oben, nach oben
urgent *59* dringend, eilig
use, to be much ~ *129* von Nutzen sein

V

value *130+* Wert
van *40* Lieferwagen
vanilla *60* Vanille
various *126* verschiedene
various *18* verschiedene
vegetable *61* Gemüse
vehicle *40+* Fahrzeug
version *60* Variante, Version
virus *72T* Virus
vocational academy *33* Berufsakademie
vocational college *33* Berufsfachschule
vocational school *30* Berufsschule
voicemail *22* Anrufbeantworter
voltage *52* (Strom-)Spannung; **high ~** *102* Hochspannung
to volunteer *33* freiwillig arbeiten, ehrenamtlich tätig sein
volunteer work *75* ehrenamtliche Tätigkeit

W

wage *30* Lohn
waiter *30* Kellner
waiting room *44* Wartezimmer
waitress *30* Kellnerin
walk *16* Spaziergang, Fußweg
wall plug *62* Dübel
walnut *60* Walnuss
wanted *30* gesucht
warehouse *10* Lager(halle)
to warm up *58* (sich) aufwärmen, warm werden
warning sign *70* Warnschild
to wash the dishes *65* (Geschirr) spülen
to waste *65* verschwenden, vergeuden
waste of time *99T* Zeitverschwendung
Watch out for …! *71* Achtung bei …!
water cooler *48* Wasserkühler
to waterski *34T* Wasserski fahren
watt(s) *53* Watt
to wave (sth) *89* (mit etw) winken
way *130* Art, Weise; **the other ~ round** *75* umgekehrt; **this ~** *6T* hier entlang
weakness *97T* Schwäche

weather *6T* Wetter
wedding *50* Hochzeit
weekday *29* Wochentag, Werktag; **on ~s** *29* wochentags, werktags
to weigh *48* wiegen
weight *41* Gewicht
welcome, You're ~. *8T* Gern geschehen. Bitte sehr.
well-being *95* Wohlbefinden, Wohlergehen
Western *88* westlich
wet *34* feucht, nass
What's up? *114* Wie geht's? Alles klar?
while *72T* Weile
whole, the ~ of *96T* ganz
wide *48* breit
width *53* Breite
willing *30* bereit, willens
to win *30* gewinnen, erhalten, bekommen
wind turbine *30* Windkraftanlage
windy *34* windig
windy breeze *30* frische Brise
wine *31T* Wein
wireless *52* drahtlos, Funk-
wish, Best ~es, *40* *(Brief:)* Mit freundlichen Grüßen
within *86* innerhalb, in
wood *52* Holz
to work long hours *30* lange/ bis spät arbeiten
work environment *67* Arbeitsumgebung, -umfeld
work placement *84* Praktikum
workbench *64+* Werkbank
worker *66* Arbeiter/in; **co-~** *122* Kollege/-in
working day *49T* Werktag
working experience *30* Berufserfahrung
workload *85* Arbeitspensum
work-related *122* arbeitsbezogen
workshop *29* Werkstatt
workspace *64* Arbeitsbereich
workstation *72* Arbeitsplatz
worried *64* beunruhigt, besorgt
to worry about sth *51* sich um etw Sorgen machen
worry, Don't ~. *97T* Keine Sorge.
written *16* schriftlich

Y

yearly *70* jährlich
you name it *50T* was es auch sei
You're welcome. *8T* Gern geschehen. Bitte sehr.
You've got a point. *125* Da hast du recht.
Yours sincerely *16* *(Brief:)* Mit freundlichen Grüßen
yummy *69* lecker

**Europass
Curriculum Vitae**

Personal Information

First name(s) / Surname	Robert Fellinger
Address(es)	Corneliusstraße 3, D-84028 Landshut, Germany
Telephone(s)	+49 871 201 295
Mobile	+49 150 7752075
E-mail	robert@fellingerfamily.de
Nationality	German
Date of birth	24 Oct 1997
Gender	male

Desired employment/ occupational field	Shop assistant at Roots Brighton

Work experience

Dates	06/2015 – present
Occupation or position held	Shop assistant
Main activities and responsibilities	Responsible for kitchenware
Name and address of employer	euroDSI GmbH, Marktplatz 4, D-84055 Rottenburg
Type of business sector	Drug store chain
Dates	09/2012 – 05/2015
Occupation or position held	Shop assistant, trainee
Main activities and responsibilities	Responsible for products in dental hygiene department
Name and address of employer	euroDSI GmbH, Marktplatz 4, D-84055 Rottenburg
Type of business sector	Drug store chain
Dates	09/2013 – present
Occupation or position held	Volunteer football trainer, youth division
Main activities and responsibilities	Responsible for training youth division in soccer
Name and address of employer	Turngemeinde Landshut
Type of business sector	Sports club

Education and training

Dates	08/2012 – 05/2015
Title of qualification awarded	Shop assistant
Principal subjects / occupational skills covered	Selling goods to customers, psychology of sales, managing a shop
Name and type of organisation providing education and training	Kaufmännische Berufsschule 2, Landshut (vocational college)
Level in national or international classification	ISCED 810

Dates	09/2007 – 07/2012 Hauptschule West, Landshut
Title of qualification awarded	Hauptschulabschluss (year 9 school leaving certificate)

Personal skills and competences

Mother tongue(s)	German
Other language(s)	English

Self-assessment European level (*)

English

Comprehension		Speaking		Writing
Listening	Reading	Spoken interaction	Spoken production	
B1*	A2	B1	A2	A2

(*) Common European Framework of References for Languages

Social skills and competences	Youth work in soccer team, course in counselling for peers
Computer skills and competences	MS Office, CASH: electronic check-outs
Artistic skills and competences	Dancing and choreographing in team
Driving licence	For cars, type B
Additional information	I have the possibility to stay with a family member in Brighton.

Es gibt kein Standard-Layout für Geschäftsbriefe in der englischsprachigen Welt. Hier haben wir den üblichen Blocksatz verwendet.

available	verfügbar
enclose	beifügen
immediately	sofort, umgehend
look forward to	sich darauf freuen
request	bitten
supply	Vorrat
urgent	dringend

A

Wenzel Wellness
Breitestraße 20
76530 Baden-Baden
Germany
Tel: +49-(0)7221-556-01
Fax: +49-(0)7221-556-10
www.wenzelff.de
info@wenzelff.de

B

C **URGENT**

D
Lombardi Bed and Breakfast
8 Raven Street
Oxfordshire
OX7 3PP
United Kingdom

E 22 June 2017

F Ref: LL/En/1

G Attn: Ms Lisa Lombardi

H Dear Ms Lombardi

I **The catalogue you requested**

J
Thank you for your interest in our products. I enclose our catalogue. I understand that you need to order supplies urgently. All of the items in the catalogue are available immediately.

After you have looked at the catalogue, I would be very happy to discuss your order with you.

I look forward to hearing from you.

K Yours sincerely
L *Phillip Riedl*

M Phillip Riedl
Sales Assistant

N Enc: catalogue

O Cc: E. Kossak, Marketing

A   Name, Adresse und weitere Kontaktinformationen des Absenders

B   Vier Leerzeilen

C   Spezielle Anmerkung, falls nötig

D   Name und Adresse des Empfängers

E   Datum

Datumsangaben

Das Datum 01.05.12 erinnert Sie vielleicht an einen schönen schulfreien Tag, den Sie einmal genossen haben, aber in anderen Ländern würde dieses Datum als der fünfte Januar gelesen. Zudem würden die Leute in einigen Ländern, z.B. in den USA, dies nicht einmal als Datum erkennen, denn sie trennen die Zahlen beim Datum mit Schrägstrichen (/) oder Bindestrichen (-), aber nie mit Punkten. Manchen Menschen, mit denen Sie einen Briefwechsel haben, könnten diese internationalen Unterschiede nicht einmal bewusst sein, also schreiben Sie das Datum am besten immer wie in dem Brief auf der gegenüberliegenden Seite.

F   Eine Bezugnahme, z.B. auf eine Bestellnummer, falls nötig

G   *Attn* ist die Abkürzung für *Attention* und entspricht dem deutschen ‚zu Händen von'. Verwenden Sie *Attn* nur, wenn bei D kein Name steht.

H   Anrede (siehe Kasten unten für weitere Informationen)

I   Betreff

J   Textkörper – Achtung: In englischsprachigen Briefen wird der erste Buchstabe großgeschrieben.

K   Schlussformel

Eine Anrede und eine Schlussformel wählen

Fürs Erste empfehlen wir Ihnen die folgenden Eröffnungs- und Schlussformeln. In der Praxis werden Sie merken, dass Ihre Geschäftspartner viele verschiedene Schlussformeln verwenden.

	Opening	Closing
Wenn Sie nicht wissen, wer den Brief lesen wird	*Dear Sir or Madam*	*Yours faithfully*
Wenn Sie den Namen der Person kennen	*Dear Mr/Ms* [Nachname]	*Yours sincerely*
Wenn es ein informeller Brief ist	*Dear* [Vorname]	*Best wishes*

L   Unterschrift des Absenders (handschriftlich) – planen Sie hierfür vier Leerzeilen ein.

M   Name und Berufsbezeichnung des Absenders (maschinenschriftlich)

N   *Enc(s)* heißt *Enclosure(s)* bzw. Anlage(n). Wenn der Umschlag nur Ihren Brief enthält, brauchen Sie diese Angabe nicht.

O   Mit *Cc* können Sie angeben, dass Sie jemandem eine Kopie des Briefes schicken.

Richtlinien für E-Mails bei der Arbeit

Formelle E-Mails

Es gibt verschiedene Gründe für formelle Schreiben. Wenn Sie einem Geschäftspartner zum ersten Mal schreiben, werden Sie fast immer einen formellen Stil wählen. Andere Gründe könnten sein, dass Sie den Empfänger nicht gut kennen oder dass Ihre Firmenkultur grundsätzlich sehr formell ist. Wenn Sie im formellen Stil schreiben, halten Sie sich am besten an die folgenden Regeln:

- Beginnen Sie Ihre E-Mail auf eine der folgenden Arten:
    - *Dear Mr/Ms* [Nachname] (wenn Sie den Namen der Person kennen)
    - *Dear Sir or Madam* (wenn Ihnen der Name nicht bekannt ist)
    - Verwenden Sie keine unnötigen Abkürzungen, z. B. *Jan.* für *January* oder *dept.* für *department*.
- Verwenden Sie Ausrufezeichen (!) nur unter extremen Umständen und verwenden Sie nie mehrere Ausrufezeichen (!!!).
- Schreiben Sie nicht in GROSSBUCHSTABEN.
- Verwenden Sie keine Smileys und keinen Internetslang wie *lol*.
- Beenden Sie Ihre E-Mail mit *Yours faithfully* (wenn Sie den Namen des Empfängers nicht wissen) oder mit *Yours sincerely* (wenn Ihnen der Name bekannt ist) sowie mit Ihrem vollständigen Namen.
- Verwenden Sie immer ein Rechtschreibprogramm.

Informelle E-Mails bei der Arbeit

In Ihrem Berufsleben wird es einige Kollegen und Geschäftspartner geben, die Sie gut kennen. Bei ihnen können Sie oft einen etwas informelleren Schreibstil verwenden, aber nicht so informell wie mit Kumpels in einem Chatroom. Es gibt trotzdem noch einige Regeln zu beachten.

- Beginnen Sie Ihre E-Mail auf eine der folgenden Arten:
    - *Dear/Hello Mr/Ms …*
    - *Dear/Hello* [Vorname]
    - *Hi* [Vorname] (sehr informell)
- Sie dürfen Ausrufezeichen verwenden, besonders wenn Sie *Thanks!* sagen wollen. Aber mehrfache Ausrufezeichen sind trotzdem nicht empfehlenswert.
- Gelegentliche Smileys sind in Ordnung, aber nicht mehr als eins pro E-Mail.
- Einige Ausdrücke des Internetslangs sind akzeptabel und manchmal sogar nützlich, z. B. *imo (in my opinion)*. Verwenden Sie aber *lol* und andere Ausdrücke, die mit Lachen zu tun haben, nur mit sehr engen Kollegen.
- Akzeptable Schlussformeln sind unter anderem *Best regards* und *Best wishes*.

Bildquellenverzeichnis

Cover: Corbis RM/Alan Schein Photography

S. 6/corbis/Tim Pannell, **S. 8**/shutterstock/Stephen Coburn, **S. 10**/1/shutterstock/erashov, **S. 10**/2/shutterstock, **S. 12**/oben/AlamyRF/Image Source/IS978, **S. 12**/1/Picture-Alliance/DeFodi, **S. 12**/2/Photoshot/A3587_Ronald Wittek, **S. 12**/3/Picture Alliance/dpa/Hubert Boesl, **S. 12**/4/Picture-Alliance, **S. 14**/Corbis/WalterHodges, **S. 18**/1/Fotofinder/imagetrust, **S. 18**/2/Fotofinder/beyond, **S. 18**/3/shutterstock/Dmitry Kalinovsky, **S. 18**/4/CorbisRF/cultura/Monty Rakusen, **S. 21**/mauritius images/VIEW pictures, **S. 22**/shutterstock/vgStudio, **S. 24**/1/shutterstock/PeterBernik, **S. 24**/2/shutterstock/MonkeyBusinessImages, **S. 25**/Fotolia/KlausEppele, **S. 26**/shutterstock/TatianaMorozova, **S. 28**/shutterstock/Maridav, **S. 30**/1/shutterstock/Warren Goldswain, **S. 30**/2/Donskaya Olga, **S. 31**/1/shutterstock/Sheftsoff, **S. 31**/2/shutterstock/qingqing, **S. 32**/shutterstock/Dmitry Kalinovsky, **S. 36**/1/Shutterstock/GaudiLab, **S. 36**/2/Fotofinder/BildagenturOnline, **S. 41**/1/shutterstock/KENCKOphotography, **S. 41**/2/shutterstock/DDCoral, **S. 41**/3/shutterstock/Fedor Selivanov, **S. 41**/4/shutterstock/Naiyyer, **S. 41**/5/shutterstock/Maksim Toome, **S. 42**/1/Depositphotos/Jim_Filim, **S. 42**/2/Depositphotos/magraphics, **S. 42**/3/Depositphotos/sunRise, **S. 42**/4/Depositphotos/vtlsdp, **S. 44**/1/shutterstock/Maksym Bondarchuk, **S. 44**/2/shutterstock/LesPalenik, **S. 44**/3/shutterstock/DJ Srki, **S. 44**/4/shutterstock/vlad_star, **S. 44**/5/shutterstock/Le Do, **S. 45**/1/shutterstock/nart, **S. 45**/2/shutterstock/nart, **S. 45**/3/shutterstock/Galushko Sergey, **S. 45**/4/shutterstock/Ljupco Smokovski, **S. 48**/1/shutterstock/Vdimitry, **S. 48**/2/shutterstock/Loskutnikov, **S. 49**/Alamy/DavidPearson, **S. 50**/shutterstock/wavebreakmedia, **S. 51**/shutterstock/K Goldenberg, **S. 52**/1/shutterstock/OleksiyMark, **S. 52**/2/shutterstock/Ministr84, **S. 52**/3/shutterstock/Lyf1, **S. 53**/1/shutterstock/Nordling, **S. 53**/2/shutterstock/Supertrooper, **S. 54**/1/McDonalds Deutschland Inc., **S. 54**/2/Skype, **S. 54**/3/Audi AG, **S. 54**/4/Nike AG, **S. 55**/1/Picture-Alliance/BerndWeissbrod, **S. 55**/2/Daimler AG, **S. 55**/3/Daimler AG, **S. 57**/shutterstock/StockLite, **S. 58**/iStock/by_nicholas, **S. 60**/1/shutterstock/VenusAngel, **S. 60**/2/ shutterstock/NataliaLisovskaya, **S. 66**/1/Fotofinder/GlobalWarmingImages, **S. 66**/2/Fotofinder/2_Weis/, **S. 66**/3/Alamy/Ali Kabas, **S. 72**/1/shutterstock/Yuri Arcurs, **S. 72**/2/shutterstock/Dmitry Kalinovsky, **S. 72**/3/shutterstock/Aletia, **S. 72**/4/shutterstock/auremar, **S. 72**/5/shutterstock/DeanBertoncelj, **S. 72**/6/shutterstock/MonkeyBusinessImages, **S. 72**/unten1/shutterstock/Yobidaba, **S. 72**/unten3/shutterstock/Maluson, **S. 72**/unten4/shutterstock/Leremy, **S. 75**/Fotofinder/allesalltag, **S. 76**/Alamy/British Retail Photography, **S. 78**/Fotofinder/Freelens, **S. 80**/Picture-Alliance/dpa/Marijan Murat, **S. 81**/Picture Alliance/dpa/Uli Deck, **S. 86**/Cartoonstock/HarleySchwadron, **S. 87**/Fotofinder/Thomas Willemsen, **S. 89**/shutterstock/Atlaspix, **S. 91**/Fotofinder/bilderbox, **S. 92**/shutterstock/lightspring, **S. 95**/1/shutterstock/StockLite, **S. 95**/2/iStock/KaiChiang, **S. 95**/3/istock/AlexanderRaths, **S. 95**/4/istock/PedroCastellano, **S. 95**/5/shutterstock/kurhan, **S. 96**/shutterstock/YuriArcurs, **S. 97**/1/shutterstock/AlexanderSysolyatin, **S. 97**/2/shutterstock/iQoncept, **S. 97**/3/shutterstock/StockLite, **S. 98**/shutterstock/anneka, **S. 104**/shutterstock/MonkeyBusinessImages, **S. 106**/AlamyRF/RadiusImages, **S. 108**/shutterstock/YuriArcurs, **S. 109**/Picture Alliance/dpa-Zentralbild/Nestor Bachmann, **S. 110**/shutterstock/OleksiyMark, **S. 111**/Fotofinder/F1online/JuiceImages, **S. 112**/1/shutterstock/AddyTsl, **S. 112**/2/shutterstock/Fotonium, **S. 112**/3/shutterstock/JustinKirkThornton, **S. 112**/4/shutterstock/NataliyaHora, **S. 112**/5/shutterstock/SergeyMironov, **S. 113**/FotoFinder/Stock4B/StefanieSudek, **S. 115**/shutterstock/Nan728, S. 116/1/shutterstock/auremar, **S. 116**/2/shutterstock/auremar, **S. 117**/1/shutterstock/Goodluz, **S. 117**/2/shutterstock/wavebreakmedia, **S. 120**/shutterstock/GeorgeGreen, **S. 121**/1/shutterstock/JohnJAMES, **S. 121**/2/shutterstock/Elena Elisseeva, **S. 123**/1/shutterstock/MandyGodbehear, **S. 123**/2/shutterstock/Fanfo, **S. 124**/FotoFinder/F1online, **S. 125**/1/shutterstock/Hadrian, **S. 125**/2/shutterstock/IgorTerekhor, **S. 126**/1/shutterstock/CharlotteLake, **S. 126**/2/shutterstock/deMingo, **S. 126**/3/shutterstock/ElenaGaak, **S. 126**/4/shutterstock/RichardSemik, **S. 126**/5/shutterstock/Vynogradova, **S. 127**/Shutterstock, **S. 128**/shutterstock/Nodokthr, **S. 129**/1/shutterstock/ChristosGeorghiou, **S. 129**/2/shutterstock/Tanderson, **S. 129**/3/shutterstock/HenriEnsio, **S. 129**/4/shutterstock/Dahotski, **S. 129**/5/shutterstock/YuryShchipakin, **S. 130**/1/Fotolia/sunnyImages, **S. 130**/2/shutterstock/DmitryKalinovsky, **S. 130**/3/shutterstock/NormanPogson, **S. 130**/4/shutterstock/wavebreakmedia, **S. 130**/5/shutterstock/TylerOlson, **S. 133**/shutterstock/Iakov Filimonov, **S. 154**/shutterstock/PaulsonPhotography

Bitte beachten Sie, dass es nicht für alle deutschen Berufsbezeichnungen eine Standardübersetzung gibt. In manchen Fällen ist es notwendig, die Arbeitsaufgaben zu beschreiben, um englischsprachigen Personen mitzuteilen, was genau man beruflich macht.

Änderungsschneider/in	alterations tailor
Altenpfleger/in	geriatric nurse
Anlagenmechaniker/in	systems mechanic
Asphaltbauer/in	asphalt worker
Automatenfachmann/-frau	vending machine expert
Automobilkaufmann/-frau	automotive sales management assistant
Automobilmechaniker/in	automobile mechanic
Bäcker/in	baker
Bankkaufmann/-frau	bank business management assistant
Bauzeichner/in	draftsman/draftswoman
Berufskraftfahrer/in	(professional) driver
Bestattungsfachkraft	undertaker
Betonfertigteilbauer/in	prefabricated concrete constructor
Beton-Stahlbetonbauer/in	concrete and reinforced concrete builder
Biologisch-technische/r Assistent/in	(biological) technician
Bürofachkraft	(skilled) office assistant
Bürokaufmann/-frau	office management assistant
Chemikant/in	chemical technician
Dachdecker/in	roofer
Diätassistent/in	dietician
Einzelhandelskaufmann/-frau	retail management assistant
Elektriker/in	electrician
Elektroanlagenmonteur/in	electrical systems fitter/ technician
Elektroniker/in	electronics technician
Ergotherapeut/in	occupational therapist
Erzieher/in	childcare teacher
Fachinformatiker/in	computer technician
Fachkraft für Lagerlogistik	management assistant in warehousing and logistics
Fachlagerist/in	(skilled) warehouse operator
Fachpraktiker/in Hauswirtschaft	professional housekeeper
Fachverkäufer/in	sales specialist
Fahrradmonteur/in	bicycle assembler
Fleischer/in	butcher
Fliesenleger/in	tile layer
Florist/in	florist
Friseur/in	hairdresser
Gärtner/in	gardener
Gerüstbauer/in	scaffolder
Großhandelskaufmann/-frau	management assistant in wholesale
Hotelfachmann/-frau	hotel industry expert, hotel clerk
Industriekaufmann/-frau	industrial management assistant
Industriemechaniker/in	industrial mechanic
IT Systemelektroniker/in	IT systems engineer
Kellner/in	waiter/waitress
Koch/Köchin	cook
Kraftfahrzeug-mechatroniker/in	automotive mechatronics technician
Krankenschwester/ Krankenpfleger	nurse
Maler/in und Lackierer/in	painter and varnisher
Maschinen- und Anlagenführer/in	machine and plant operator
Medizinischer/r Fachangestellte/r	physician's assistant
Mechatroniker/in	mechatronic technician
Mediengestalter/in	audiovisual media designer
Metallbauer/in	metalworker
Physiotherapeut/in	physiotherapist
Polizist/in	police officer
Restaurantfachmann/-frau	(skilled) restaurant worker
Soldat/in	soldier
Speditionskaufmann/-frau	freight forwarding management assistant
Sport- und Fitnesskaufmann/-frau	sport and fitness management assistant
Tierpfleger/in	animal keeper
Tischler/in	carpenter
Veranstaltungskaufmann/ -frau	event management assistant
Verkäufer/in	salesperson
Verwaltungsfachangestellte/r	skilled administrative assistant
Veterinärmedizinisch-technische/r Assistent/in	veterinary technician
Werkzeugmechaniker/in	tool mechanic, tool engineer
Zerspanungsmechaniker/in	metal cutting mechanic

REMEMBER

I want to be **a** salesperson.
I'm going to be **an** auto mechanic.